WOUND BUILDING

Before you start to read this book, take this moment to think about making a donation to punctum books, an independent non-profit press,

@ https://punctumbooks.com/support/

If you're reading the e-book, you can click on the image below to go directly to our donations site. Any amount, no matter the size, is appreciated and will help us to keep our ship of fools afloat. Contributions from dedicated readers will also help us to keep our commons open and to cultivate new work that can't find a welcoming port elsewhere. Our adventure is not possible without your support.

Vive la Open Access.

Fig. 1. Hieronymus Bosch, *Ship of Fools* (1490–1500)

WOUND BUILDING: DISPATCHES FROM THE LATEST DISASTERS IN UK POETRY. Copyright © 2021 by Danny Hayward. This work carries a Creative Commons BY-NC-SA 4.0 International license, which means that you are free to copy and redistribute the material in any medium or format, and you may also remix, transform and build upon the material, as long as you clearly attribute the work to the authors (but not in a way that suggests the authors or punctum books endorses you and your work), you do not use this work for commercial gain in any form whatsoever, and that for any remixing and transformation, you distribute your rebuild under the same license. http://creativecommons.org/licenses/by-nc-sa/4.0/

First published in 2021 by punctum books, Earth, Milky Way.
https://punctumbooks.com

ISBN-13: 978-1-68571-000-2 (print)
ISBN-13: 978-1-68571-001-9 (ePDF)

DOI: 10.53288/0322.1.00

LCCN: 2021947625
Library of Congress Cataloging Data is available from the Library of Congress

Book design: Vincent W.J. van Gerven Oei
Cover image: Lucy Beynon

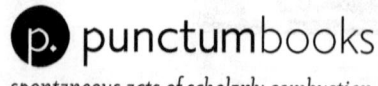

spontaneous acts of scholarly combustion

HIC SVNT MONSTRA

Danny Hayward

Wound Building
Dispatches from the Latest Disasters in UK Poetry

p.

Contents

Preface · 15

1. Ingrown Expressionism:
On Frances Kruk and Verity Spott · 29

2. Strong Language:
On Lucy Beynon and Lisa Jeschke · 45

3. Class Separation vs. Separation Anxiety:
A Brief Psychotic Interlude · 61

4. Transgression for Anti-Fascists:
On Verity Spott · 71

5. World History's Teenage Diaries:
On Lisa Jeschke · 91

6. Poetry and Self-Defense:
On Xu Lizhi and Nat Raha · 115

7. Wound Building: On T.S. Eliot, Amiri Baraka, Bernadette Mayer, and Keston Sutherland · 133

8. Mood Music for Wound Building
(Some Working Notes on Immediacy) · 157

9. "Language is for Fucking Idiots":
On Porpentine Charity Heartscape · 165

10. Letter to Lotte L.S.:
On Sean Bonney · 183

Bibliography · 201

Acknowledgments

I'm glad to be able to publish these essays together because they present a broader account of the culture that makes them possible than any of the pieces could individually. Nevertheless, the account leaves almost everyone out. Thanks to: Paul Abbott, Larne Abse Gogarty, Tom Allen, Jacob Bard-Rosenberg, John Barker, Jasper Bernes, Tom Betteridge, Lucy Beynon, Hannah Black, Sharon Borthwick, Anne Boyer, Andrea Brady, Anja Buechele, Simon Bull, Toby Bull, David Buuck, Stuart Calton, Sophie Carapetian, Christina Chalmers, Maria Chehonadskih, Joshua Clover, Jennifer Cooke, John Cunningham, Miri Davidson, Darsavini, Nia Davies, Gloria Dawson, Amy De'ath, Cole Denyer, Helen Dimos, Caitlin Doherty, Sam Dolbear, Ines Doujak, Lucy Duncan, Steve Edwards, Robbie Ellen, Cierán Finlayson, Joey Frances, Antony Francis, Ulli Freer, Jackqueline Frost, Johnny Gallagher, Melanie Gilligan, Harry Gilonis, James Goodwin, Alva Gotby, David Grundy, Rose-Anne Gush, Chris Gutkind, Matt Hall, Rob Halpern, Ayesha Hameed, Richard Hames, Jeremy Hardingham, Edmund Hardy, Ian Heames, Caspar Heinemann, Rosa van Hensbergen, Jeff Hilson, Lizzie Homersham, Gabriel Humberstone, Anthony Iles, Lisa Jeschke, Sacha Kahir, Justin Katko, Robert Kiely, Laura Kilbride, Frances Kruk, Ashok Kumar, Johnny Liron, Francesca Lisette, Rona Lorimer, Lotte L.S., Rob Lucas, Ed Luker, Joe Luna, Mira Mattar, Marianne Morris, Paige Murphy, Jeff Nagy, Daniel Neofetou, Sean O'Brien, Gizem Okulu, Andrew Osborne, Rich Owens, David Panos, Tony Paraskeva, Richard Parker, Neil Pattison,

Alexei Penzin, Nell Perry, Holly Pester, Malcolm Phillips, Hannah Proctor, Jèssica Pujol Duran, Wail Qasim, Nat Raha, Nisha Ramayya, Ash Reid, Luke Roberts, Will Rowe, Tim Savage, Connie Scozzaro, Ben Seymour, Azad Sharma, Kashif Sharma Patel, Sam Solomon, Juliana Spahr, Verity Spott, Kerstin Stakemeier, Eirik Steinhoff, Keston Sutherland, Zoe Sutherland, Paul Sutton, Timothy Thornton, Cassandra Troyan, Hector Uniacke, Florence Uniacke, Laurel Uziell, Nikhil Vettukattil, Marina Vishmidt, Juha Virtanen, Mike Wallace-Hadrill, Jo Walton, Sam Walton, Clinical Wasteman, Emilia Weber, Naomi Weber, Steve Willey, Kyle Zeto, all my comrades in the London Renters Union, No Money, Tories Out, Save Ridley Road, and anyone else who I've momentarily forgotten. Also to Kristen McCants for the copyediting, and to Vincent and Eileen at punctum for their brilliant refusal of publishing industry norms.

I particularly owe Luke Roberts, Francesca Lisette, and Ed Luker, for bailing me out, repeatedly, and Lucy Beynon for the cover image. Thank you to David Buuck, Group for Conceptual Politics, David Grundy, and Florence Uniacke for publishing earlier versions of some of these essays, and to Lotte for writing back.

Marina Vishmidt has for many years gently explained to me the thing about "readers."

Love and solidarity to all.

*The tongue can make
something break
or it can heal*

— Kojo Kanjam

I doubt it's possible to produce many spontaneous (or elaborated) images of this kind without concentrating the mind on this production — a concentration that can only harm thought in general.

— Victor Serge

Preface

"For one another" is our name for Wound Building

This is a book about some people. I could say that it's a book about poetry, but in the time it has taken me to write it I've become less interested in the meaning of the separation between the writing and the lives that give rise to it. Its chapters focus on one group of poets (almost all of whom are known to one another) active in a self-organizing poetry scene in the UK in the period from 2010 until today. Most of them discuss poems with little to no audience outside of the scene of their producers, the little magazines that they publish, and the reading series that they put on. In the early parts of the book I am still ostentatiously engaged in presenting "literary criticism" of these writings. In the later ones, not so much.

The poetry is generally violent. When I wrote the first draft of this introduction I claimed that it becomes more conscious of this fact as time passes, but now that I've gone back and read the essays through I'm not sure that the opposite isn't the case. What begins as an overtly self-aware poetry of crassness and brutality over time becomes crass and violent by habit and educated instinct. Violence gets turned more frequently back against the self, but it doesn't follow from this that we are also more conscious of it.

I think now that violence and crassness have been our Romanticism, our sexual liberation, our freedom movement, in the sense of the one thing that it feels most possible to realize and make beautiful and intellectually persuasive. The poets I discuss here write violent love poems and violent elegies as well as violent fantasies composed in stabs of violent verse and violent prose. They write crass poems for one another full of violent images, and they are unable to explain why they do this except that they feel at some level as if the violence were solidarity and the crassness mutual aid, and their violent little magazines and journals carry essays on this feeling of which the crassest passages and equivocations make us think it's true.

It's not a mystery. We've wanted to write about things that are unarguable, that are basic to our experience. We've wanted to give one another new ways of expressing just how unarguable and how basic they are. If we teach one another to be impatient, breathless, and illogical in language, it's because there are more important things in life than the length of our attention spans and the conceptual niceness of our reasoning. If we've made art that is crass, stupid, and unthinking, it's because we've wanted solidarity and mutual aid to be audible in language as shitty, impulsive, and emotionally immature as ourselves (and because nothing in the world makes us happier than when it is). We have been violent for one another and idiotic for one another, and sometimes even murderous for one another; but throughout all of it we've retained the common decency not to be beautiful.

The individual chapters were written between April 2015 and February 2020. The poems they talk about are fantasies of the murder of David Cameron, dreams of being split open along a seam, basement songs, hundreds of pages of notes on working life in a privatized care home in Hove, East Sussex, a four-line slogan about the Cologne groping scandal of New Year 2016, variations on the *Refugees Medical Phrasebook,* a life wasted in a factory in Guangzhou, ~~of permanence,~~ an autobiographical sci-fi internet fever dream, an anarchist elegy, and a refusal to argue. And I was going to try to say something sensible here about the historical "context" of this writing, and about what we've been responding to, but one of the lessons the poems have taught me is never to write worthy narrative when it seems like a fucked up collage will do.

I used to think that this might be a book about Marxism and poetry. Insofar as the early chapters have an argument, it has to do with this question. I wanted to make a claim about what a Marxist poetry might do, or be. Inevitably this entailed an argument about what it should reject, or despise. It might be worth just presenting a sketch of that, if only for safekeeping.

Anyone who is familiar with contemporary art or poetry will be familiar with work that recasts itself as a kind of commentary on the outputs of the culture industry. Poetry that is about recent pop music, or that becomes a kind of never-ending gloss on pop lyrics that stand in for the total affective accomplishment of the work with which they are associated, is now a familiar tendency within admired and institutionally recognized literature and is written by authors of very diverse basic political tendencies. Work of this kind is, I think, implicitly hostile to self-initiated artistic activity on realistic social grounds, whether these are consciously recognized and theoretically asserted or tacitly presupposed and merely internalized. The claim to which they assent is that the division of social labor means that only capital-initiated art can lay claim to primary transformative social affects, and that art that is self-organized or self-initiated is condemned to serve either as a kind of inquiry into the historical meaning of those affects, or at best as a kind of intelligent model of how they might be received, cognized, and diversified into instinct and habitual orientation. For art of this kind, the specialization of self-initiated artmaking represents a kind of destiny, which is just one version of the destiny of educated middle-class people in the West to be assimilated into the economy's tertiary or service sectors.

As a way of thinking about poetry, "Marxism" for me has meant identifying work whose producers have tried, not to measure their writing against a body of poems in a canon or predecessor tradition, but against the prevailing social standard of capital-initiated culture more generally. For authors of this poetic tendency, writing that is content to imagine its significance in relation to the history of poetry as an institution is dumb shit: the complacent niche-formation undertaken by those who are content either diligently to ignore the larger development of a capital-dependent culture, or else — what is now the more respectable current, even in the catalogues of arch-conservative UK poetry publishing houses — to shore up their position in relation to it by reimagining the form in which they are working as a kind of institutionalized space for reflection on that which they are incapable of meaningfully replicating. Marxism for me has therefore amounted to something like an attitude. Its practical class consciousness is defined first and foremost by a desire to match up to a capital-dependent culture and the sensations in which it traffics: it is the desire to be moving against the odds. Its materialism is defined first and foremost by the effort to be as engaging as work that relies on an entirely different division of social labor.[1] These definitions are clearly polemical, underdeveloped, and suggestive, and the

---

1   I think that the following passage of Simone White's *Dear Angel of Death*, which is not speaking about class but about black life in the United States, and therefore about an overwhelmingly proletarianized minority living under the specific trauma of slavery and white supremacism, lucidly articulates what I can only bowdlerize with reference to a more general case: "I'm saying, or rather, asking, isn't it possible that the complex knit of song and people, today, confesses a contraction in the imagination of freedom from the status of property, plunging headlong into the terrifying convergence of blackness with capital the likes of which we have never seen and have not begun to understand? Rap music in the new formation invites motivated consumers — there is no distinction here between artist and consumer, there is no distinction here between the sacred black (male) expurgation of the inauthentic R&B-type lame forms of emotion and the invitation to simulate/sample/make copies of the raw or real or 'true' experience of the black, or black life, such as Murda Beatz [...] — to participate in ritual conflation of 'enjoyment' with disgust": Simone White, *Dear Angel of Death* (New York: Ugly Duckling Presse, 2018), 136. I have written about this book in "Tradition vs. Grid: Simone White's *Dear Angel of Death*," *Texte zur Kunst* 117 (March 2020): 168–76.

most valuable poetry could very easily be written by people who violently disagree with them.

In any case, the passage to this kind of experience of poetry's tasks is necessarily circuitous. It leads out of the scene of poetry as a subculture, in which a small group of people are able to experience disruptions in the organization of language as a deep insight into social reality, and into the wider world of capital-initiated culture, in which not only the dominant ideas but also the dominant sensations are organized by means of the investment of an inordinate amount of technical proficiency and expertise. There is no way back towards a meaningful belief in the power of poetry to move people on its own terms that does not face into this capital-initiated culture and attempt to come to terms with it. The expressive insignificance of the declamatory political poetry of, say, the 1930s is at least partly due to the fact that, in the 2020s, the affects for which it aims all possess, in Marx's terms, a specific technical composition, which is to say a level of development defined by all of the materials and techniques that go into the production of capitalist art. Good poetry now being written might usefully be considered in these terms, and in some of the earlier chapters of this book, this is how I try to consider it.

One final point before I summarize the individual chapters. If there is a more specific reason for the emergence of a countertendency to the ideology of immobilization in poetry, which is to say to the idea that there is nothing for poetry to do other than reflect on capital-initiated culture, then this has to do with the transformations of language as a whole. Popular linguistic practice has altered in so many ways in the past decade and a half that it is maddening to try to keep up with it. It changes faster than experience. Its idioms change, its grammars change, its orthographies change, its phonological attack changes. In the last five years its structural meta-languages have changed, in line with the technical requirements of corporate data platforms. Its rhymes, scale, fonts, colors, and music have changed, at the initiative of Facebook and Google (the latter now incorporated as Alphabet, Inc., in open acknowledgement of its claims on the total ensemble of the means of human communication viewed from the ground-level right up to its gyrus in the Cloud). Whether we can drag our earlier political certainties kicking and screaming through the scene of all of this verbiage remains unclear. I want to do that, as I think that critics such as the Wealth of Negations group and the poet Simone White have already done for the materials of corporate managerial jargon and contemporary rap respectively. But in any event poetry remains an obvious candidate to measure up the historical cataclysms in its medium.[2]

I have called the volume *Wound Building* because this is the best phrase that I know of for the dominant aesthetics, which is to say the aesthetics under whose shadow any group of counter-practitioners will have to live and work. It isn't a name for a particular genre or group of artists, for instance for the many writers whom I discuss in depth in what follows — in particular Frances Kruk, Verity Spott, Lucy Beynon, Lisa Jeschke, Xu Lizhi, Nat Raha, Keston Sutherland, Porpentine Charity Heartscape, Lotte L.S., and Sean Bonney — nor is it a shorthand for the many whom I might have done, from the various groups of authors now published by Commune Editions in the US, or by Materials, Shit Valley, Barque Press, 87 Press, and Veer in the UK, or by a multitude of radical poetry journals such as *Tripwire*, *Materials*

---

2 The logic of this transformation of the medium is itself disarmingly simple. Large capitalist interests subcontract to hundreds of thousands of enterprising individuals the tasks of breaking up our syntax, increasing the turnover of our idioms, retrenching the extent of our paragraphs, and flattening out our rhymes, on pain of disappearance from the structures of visibility over which those interests have established a complete and lucrative monopoly. Over time, whole new structures of linguistic expectation are sunk into our heads like concrete pilings. And what is so challenging about this orgy of competitive reductionism is not the explanation for it, which is, when all is said and done, not so very different from the explanation for the restructuring of the taxi trade. Its challenge is rather that it is carried on with an energy of such breathtaking and desperate intensity that it can sometimes feel in the midst of it distractingly similar to revolutionary ardor.

(again), *Splinter*, *Lana Turner Journal*, *Armed Cell*, or *Datableed*.[3] It is, instead, a name for the limits that we all run up against: the constraints of a capitalist culture that is itself constrained to sublimate the real suffering and disappointment that it produces and reproduces. In this sense, it is the name for a context, in the same way that the Iraq war is a context, or transnational austerity is a context, which is to say that it is simply the reality to which we are compelled to construct an alternative. Sublime woundedness, the impressions of wounds opening up like LED-lit shopfronts in the night, in a parallel universe in which injury is intoxicatingly impersonal and structural, is the environment in which the poems that I discuss in this book fight to absolutize the value of every last breath; or face into the reality of extravagantly violent wish fulfilment; or dissolve themselves in search of new ways of professing love; or transform into a kind of expressionism the vomiting up of medical-diagnostic categories founded in abstract social labor; or pump their verses full of the convulsive rhythms of surprise and sudden relief, without any guarantee that this is the right thing to do or that anyone will even fucking hear. Historicizing criticism shows this kind of thing in retrospect, and admires it for its aesthetic strategies. Criticism written in the spirit of the work itself tries to get across some of the immediate sense of what it makes possible.

As I said earlier, the chapters were written at different times and in response to changing conjunctures. Some of the earlier ones treat the poems they discuss as a way to speak about a theoretical argument about art and technique, to give an account of how an individualist mode like poetry could have a relation to that. In particular, the first chapter, "Ingrown Expressionism," responds to the re-emergence of cybernetic and post-humanist programs for "post"-capitalism in the wake of the Tory re-election in 2015. By way of two short readings of the poets Frances Kruk and Verity Spott, and their own writing on the technical

---

[3] Intense collectivized attention is one form of mutual aid, and we absolutely don't care who sneers at that conviction.

management of interior life, it makes the case for the integral unity of expressionist art and the most advanced developments in capitalist technique, and it denies the separation of convenience between progressive technology, on the one hand, and regressive will, passion, and instinct, on the other.

How is poetry capable of responding to these developments? Anyone who has a sense of the current meanings of that category will be skeptical as to the premises of the question. The term is incomparably underspecified. It refers to a moribund heritage industry dominated by conservative nostalgists, to a history of spoken performance, and to any form of language art that falls outside of the domain of the equally inert form of the commercial novel. As a concept encompassing a sort of boring aesthetic provincialism and a negative definition, it groups together practitioners who in their formal commitments are not only widely different, but who are in fact emphatically mutually hostile. Definitions of poetry "as such" are a kind of centralized arbitration for aesthetics. They are exercises in managing hostility whether they realize it or not. By contrast, the essays in this volume are not a commentary on poetry but on a loose group of mostly non-institutionally supported artists trying frantically to respond to their own personal and historical circumstances. The question in which they are more interested than the general one about what poetry is or can do, is how does a mode of literary production that continues to be premised mostly on individual composition face up to a cultural and social reality in which advanced division of labor is the norm? Anyone who has been bored at a poetry reading, watching an endless series of individual readers trying to compensate for their poems by way of violence of address or ostentation of clown shoes, will have an idea of the problem. All of the writers who I discuss in this book have dealt with it in their own ways.

The second chapter, on the theatrical work of Lucy Beynon and Lisa Jeschke, focuses on two writers who have taken the simple and unusual step of trying to deal with it by means of sustained collaboration. It also presents a recognizably theoretical argument, in this case in relation to Wilhelm Reich's account of the enfeeblement of the fascist subject; and it pursues Reich's trail of clues all the way into the establishment theory of the virtuous moral neutrality of the literary imagination, on which Knights and Dames of the British Empire can be found neutrally expatiating in the pages of the *London Review of Books*. The earliest of the chapters by date of composition, it also deals with the text that is most self-consciously and intelligently violent: Beynon and Jeschke's play is among many other things also a sort of abstract of the thinking that has been carried on in an entire shared culture about the nature of political violence, and it remains poised, ambivalently, at the boundary of other forms of violence less intelligently cognized and articulated.

At the center of this book, cleaving silently through the middle of it, is a social fact that is only glancingly discussed in much of the poetry it deals with. This is obviously the emergence in the dead center of public consciousness of Donald Trump, in the four years leading up to his pseudo-insurrection and provisional suppression by Facebook and Twitter.

In the period beginning with the announcement of Trump's campaign for the US presidency, there was an unstoppable outpouring of analyses of his politics, the politics of his supporters, their online ecosystems, their aesthetics, their styles of dress, their music, and their culture. Every word that proceeded from the mouth of a white cis man was squeezed for every last ounce of cultural outrage-value. The most unspeakably commonplace grad-student name-dropping was treated as if it disclosed the deepest secrets of Western culture from its origination in the Greek *agora* to this afternoon in Mar-a-Lago. Almost none of the people who took it upon themselves to write about those topics tried to think seriously about emancipatory, anti-fascist culture or to take seriously the art of those who are working consciously to produce it.

Most of the poetry discussed from Chapter 3 onwards works within this conjuncture, and the core of the book is taken up by studies of poets for whom the re-emergent fascism of the post-2015 period went off in their thinking like a bomb. It shows them changing. Chapter 3 presents a brief thematic interlude on aesthetics and class politics written during the week of Trump's inauguration. Chapter 4, "Transgression for Anti-Fascists," on Verity Spott's long poem-cum-worker's inquiry *Click Away Close Door Say*, preoccupies itself with the most consciously aesthetic term to be used in the defense of renascent authoritarianism. The chapter presents a reconstruction of Spott's poem's singular representation of mental breakdown and capitalist restructuring, a derangement of the senses in the age of Ctrl-X + Ctrl-V, a collage scattered to the brink of despair. It tries, not only to explain some of the things that make the poem worth reading, but also to reproduce in high resolution some of its almost inexplicable urgency: the unrelenting distinctiveness of its attempt to retrieve from the claustrophobic everyday surroundings of a destroyed and destructive workplace the intellectual resources with which to understand a fascist reality that might at first seem, and here and there really is, but finally would only like to be, its spectacular counter-pole or opposite.

In my view Spott's anti-fascist art is not defined simply by the reactive attempt to reclaim for "the left" the mantle of a transgressive counterculture that "the right" has usurped. It is, instead, an attempt to see more deeply into the reality of social violence than fascist provocateurs can even dream of, and to countenance in that process of inquiry a possibility of error, or failure, or catastrophic moral misjudgment, that they would not be able to bear. Criticism that tries to extract from writing like this only the quintessence of its explanation of concepts like transgression or fascism panders to an authoritarianism that even at its most pantomime-irrationalist remains deeply incapable of risking the sensation of public error or exposure.

And as such her work also marks out a more general transition. Poets who began to write blisteringly, single-mindedly violent work about politicians around the time that Sean Bonney summed it all up — "But now, surprise attack by a government of millionaires"[4] — begin to write woundingly, distractingly vio-

---

[4] Sean Bonney, "Letter on Poetics," in *Happiness: Poems after Rimbaud* (London: Unkant, 2011), 65.

lent work as the authority of that government enters into decline.⁵ Violence is turned against the self or shredded into tissues of improbable description. Ideas that enter into the world as the sun that colors and warms it progressively deteriorate into the misshapen punching-bag of a mind that has no other use for them. In what sense is this poetry anti-fascist? Is it even meaningfully political?

Answering these questions is the main aim of Chapter 4, "World History's Teenage Diaries," on Lisa Jeschke's *The Anthology of Poems by Drunk Women*. I argue that Jeschke's crude, diminished, self-cancelling poems are the most brilliant manifestation of the principle that crassness can be a form of mutual aid. Where Spott's *Click Away Close Door Say* presents a vast, shifting canvas of rivalrous impulses, the poems in Jeschke's *Anthology* are more often pared down to their most ridiculous extremities and residues. Her work is not a continuation but the inversion of Dadaist acting out, because its main purpose is not to shock some real or notional bourgeoisie, but to hurt, embarrass, and expose the real living person Lisa Jeschke, who is the author of her own most vitriolic assaults on middle-class

---

5 On the development in Bonney's own writing, see the remarks by David Grundy on his blog *Streams of Expression*: "But this does not mean that defeat is total. Bonney's recent work charts what it is like to live in conditions of defeat, of crisis, of terror, yet it manages to manifest a hope which does not refuse pessimism, does not refuse sorrow, does not refuse suffering. As he has recently written: 'It puts me in mind of a poem by Ingeborg Bachmann, where she speaks of exile, of feeling like a dead person, of languages that you can't understand passing through you like ghosts. And I guess those ghosts exist at the point where "tradition" and "strangeness" meet, where all that is defined and foul and murdered and imprisoned becomes synonymous with all that is still uncharted and unexplained and wonderful.' Bonney's poems are like that. Like 'marks on a calendar' or 'the beginnings of a map,' they are vital indices of where we are." See David Grundy, "David Grundy's Intro to My Cambridge Reading," *Gods of the Plague*, March 14, 2018, https://godsoftheplague.tumblr.com/post/171865396568/david-grundys-intro-to-my-cambridge-reading. See also David's more recent essay "Sean Bonney's Life Work," *Poetry Foundation*, March 9, 2020, https://www.poetryfoundation.org/harriet/2020/03/sean-bonneys-life-work.

propriety and gender norms and, like all of us, the frustrated bearer of exactly those same values. Her work shocks and hurts us only by this indirect route, which is to say through its passionate identification with a set of blatantly bad options.

The next two chapters adopt a slightly wider angle and try to set out some working heuristics. Chapter 5, "Poetry and Self-Defense," considers the relationship between the poetry of the British poet Nat Raha and the Chinese poet Xu Lizhi, who was famous for a day or two in 2014 when he became one of many workers at the Taiwanese-Chinese manufacturing firm Foxconn to kill himself by jumping off a building. The chapter tries to describe the defensiveness of Xu Lizhi's poetry, and it defines self-defense in art as the obstinate, reactive overvaluation of whatever it is in your life that the dominant social relation (your boss) values at nothing. Nat Raha also writes defensive poetry, and Verity Spott sometimes writes it too: the tendency amounts to a thick streak of obstinacy in the writing of those who have been hurt or have seen those whom they love hurt unnecessarily. It is a class tone susceptible to constant development and elaboration, and it remains, in the paved and well-lit environment of what the great majority of people are now made to think that poetry is, almost completely inaudible.

Chapter 7 talks about what is audible in contemporary poetry. I argue that its dominant idiom, and the dominant idiom of plenty of other art-forms as well, involves a kind of non-specific invocation of trauma, and that the idiom is so developed and so ubiquitous in the culture that it breaks in upon the work even of those writers who are conscious of it and who regard it with political disdain. The chapter sketches some stages of the idiom's ascent, from a special mode of upper bourgeois literary disillusionment to the sound that you just heard come out of that car that drove by. Via a discussion of Amiri Baraka, Bernadette Mayer, Jayne Cortez, and Keston Sutherland, it tries to figure out some of the idiom's uses.

The material here completes a gradual drift that began in the earlier chapters. The move is away from psychoanalysis-talk and its conceptual payloads of repression and disinhibition, and towards a discussion of the meaning of aesthetic "immediacy," a word the exact significance of which I don't pretend to understand. Chapter 8 presents some working notes on that concept, in order to make it as confusing as possible. Chapter 9 takes a detour into the computer games of the US-based game designer and writer Porpentine Charity Heartscape, who in her own description of her art has developed one way of thinking about what "immediacy" in poetry might be:

> I don't really know a lot about abstract concepts. I only know about the stuff I'm interested in or the tiny hyper-specific details that I focus on.[6]

The final chapter, Chapter 10, is a last, crass attempt at a summary. It takes the form of a letter to the poet Lotte L.S. written after the death of Sean Bonney, the writer whose own crassness and violence in language has provided perhaps the single greatest example of solidarity and mutual aid for the development of the poets that this book is about. The letter corrects some earlier mistakes, and adds a few more to the bonfire. I try to say more accurately what it is that I mean when I say that I am interested in poetry that hates its own ideas and wants to see the world diminished. At the time of writing I still think that this is a kind of love poetry, and that I might finally be able to show in what way.

The aim of this collection is quite limited. It is not to propose a fully cohesive account of what the poetry is, to inaugurate a "School," or to contribute to the boring tittle-tattle that for decades has constituted the great aesthetic debates of British poetry as an institution. I don't care about any of that. I care about these poems. I could barely love anything without them; and this book is a front-line report on the local detail of their latest disasters. Think of it as a travel guide.

---

6 Alexander Iadarola, "Interview with Game Designer Porpentine Charity Heartscape," *Mask Magazine*, May 29, 2017, http://www.maskmagazine.com/the-greatest-hits-issue/work/porpentine-charity-heartscape-reprise.

1

Ingrown Expressionism: On Frances Kruk and Verity Spott

In our present phase of the history of aesthetics, which some of our most prominently advertised theorists have declared to be effectively post-capitalist, many actions cost less to perform than ever. Contemporary cultural production both inside and out of cultural-industrial contexts is painfully overdetermined by the abundance of available means. Text and musical elements that once could only be produced by means of laborious training can now be sampled or cut and pasted without significant expenditure of effort. Bodies of work that previously might have seemed unapproachably arcane can now be glossed instantly by means of search commands. The resources of expressive art have never been cheaper, the productivity of the individual expressive artist has never been higher, the accomplishment of a density of surface effects in contemporary artworks has never been easier to bring about.[1] These and similar visionary procla-

---

1 Thanks to Christina Chalmers, Larne Abse Gogarty, and Marina Vishmidt for comments and criticisms. A number of the abovemtioned truisms can be found, for example, here: "The Big Dicdata — Coming Data-regimes: Currently a competition is taking place between secret service agencies and transnational corporations for the control of the main resource of our time: data. New forms of data-driven and automatized governments are arising. DISCREET promotes projects to better understand this automated

mations cost very little to say and tell us more or less nothing about the expressive situation of the individual contemporary artist. This omission can be justified on several grounds: firstly because, as John Cage wrote in 1992 (the erratic capitalization is his own), the "artist's proper behavior / SElf- / expression" should "be Put aside" for a change; or because, as Cage went on to say in the same lecture, "we hAve extended / the centRal nervous / sysTem/electrOnics   our technology / makes the reVolution for us"; or more probably for some combination of the two positions, for instance because excessive preoccupation with "the self" tends to distract artists from the major "revolutionary" developments of our period, in ICT or Computational Finance or the microprocessor industry or whatever.[2] The position is self-evidently a reflex response to the decline of socialist politics and mounts a directly political argument about how that decline may be reversed. Its advocates can concede that recent "access-driven"[3] revolutions in the means of circulating and reproducing informational goods, which according to the theoreticians of post-capitalism are now "corroding the market's ability to form prices correctly,"[4] are inseparable from, and in some cases are straightforwardly identical with, "access-driven" revolutions in the categorization and treatment of what are deemed to be dysfunctional bodies and inoperative minds.

---

future, providing improbable models and algorithmic alternatives in order to disrupt this seemingly irreversible development towards increased welfare." The last word here is either a disgrace or a disgraceful parapraxis. DIS Magazine, "DISCREET Call for Participants," *discover: the dis blog,* April 11, 2016, http://dismagazine.com/blog/81659/discreet-call-for-participants/.

2   John Cage, "Overpopulation and Art," in *Composed in America,* eds. Marjorie Perloff and Charles Junkerman (Chicago: University of Chicago Press, 1994), 36.

3   "Around the world, a new wave of peer-to-peer, access-driven businesses is shaking up established categories." PricewaterhouseCoopers, "The Sharing Economy," *Consumer Intelligence Series,* 2015, https://www.pwc.com/us/en/technology/publications/assets/pwc-consumer-intelligence-series-the-sharing-economy.pdf.

4   Paul Mason, *Postcapitalism: A Guide to Our Future* (London: Penguin, 2015), 3.

And they can blandly accept that the people who celebrate these developments most overtly are not typically the ones who are tracked cheaply by their parole officers or pressed under the thumb of a scientific diagnostic category whose definition emerges from the International Statistical Classification of Diseases.[5] They can agree that all of these facts are obvious and still hold that they are nevertheless of very minor political significance, or even that excessive concern with them is antithetical to radical politics, insofar as it justifies and entrenches a reactive aversion to the technical developments that are the true historical basis for any meaningful new anti-capitalism. New theorists of anti-capitalist rationalism might also claim that they have progressed beyond the Cagean claim that "our technology / makes the reVolution for us." Their reason for doing so would be straightforward. Their work is not avowedly quietist but, on the contrary, mounts a concerted attack on the absence of strategic political thinking on the revolutionary left. For the writers who represent this tendency, the necessity of abandoning endless in-group subcultural left squabbling so as to take a place at the great roundtable of modern managerial scientific discourse has been, from its earliest articulation, a central motif. And for the cultural improvers looking to warrant their truancy from the sub-culture, the motif has proved breathtakingly congenial.[6] But the cybernetic automatism that Cage was at least candid enough

---

5   The argument could also be made in slightly different terms. Since the rise in capitalist technical productivity has led to the conversion of the dominant psychology into a quantitative-technical discipline, the conviction that subjective expression of lived trauma might be opposed to bourgeois forms has also significantly declined in prevalence. Trauma is now itself a highly formalized medical category, theoretically integrated in a neurology of chemical pathways and socially controlled by means of a number of behavioral disciplines of varying complexity and intrusiveness. Aesthetic categories that were more or less suitable for an earlier stage of bourgeois social relations were true only because of the relative rudimentariness of the forces of production to which they corresponded. As the following will argue, in much recent expressive poetic writing this fact makes itself known intuitively and in practice.

6   See, e.g., Nick Srnicek and Alex Williams, *Inventing the Future: Postcapitalism and a World without Work* (London: Verso, 2015), 11.

to avow openly is reproduced in this newer body of work in modified form, by means of a kind of studiously over-conceptualized indifference to the actual psychic life of the agents of any possible revolutionary political transformation. Theoretical accounts of the hegemonic interpellation of the subject by a radical modernist program, in which the life of the person who is slated to be interpellated is never expressively inhabited,[7] or of conceptual virality,[8] or of the mysterious "hyperstition" of ideas strenuously imagineered by left-futurists,[9] and obligingly retweeted by left-internet users, do not cancel out this indifference but merely raise it up to a higher power, so that every gesture towards the realization of a given political strategy only fortifies at the level of political theory a pre-existing disinclination. The disinclination is as rationalist as any other obsessive compulsive disorder and as new as middle-class subjectivity itself, and phobic personalities as diverse as Sigmund Freud's Ratman and the Parliamentary Labour Party's Ramsay MacDonald have provided it with a long and distinguished cultural history. Its manifest aesthetic content is a fundamental theoretical aversion to entering into the joys and the wounds of those whose lives are actually fucked up by capital, which is to say, in other words, that it is an indifference to the living process of politics in intense and confusing human communicative exchange as this is mediated by the historical conditions of everyday personal experience. It is also an indifference to the process by which political ideas get absorbed, challenged, misunderstood, broken down, and spat back out into new and compromised

---

7 Ibid., 170ff.
8 See Cornelia Sollfrank and Rachel Baker, "Revisiting the Future with Laboria Cuboniks: A Conversation," *Furtherfield,* July 27, 2016, https://www.furtherfield.org/revisiting-the-future-with-laboria-cuboniks-a-conversation/.
9 Srnicek and Williams, *Inventing the Future,* 71–75. A clearer account of "hyperstition" is presented by the Laboria Cuboniks group, in the interview cited in the last note. Elsewhere the same group present an accurate if cautious criticism of the concept: DIS Magazine, "Laboria Cuboniks in Conversation," *discover: the dis blog,* July 23, 2016, http://dismagazine.com/blog/81953/laboria-cuboniks-in-conversation/.

environments of living conflict; to practical disagreement, misrecognition, wounded pride, escalation in struggle, the collective need in the breach for violent hyperbole and theoretical distortion; and so in short to the whole dynamic of social transformation that turns a gradualist struggle into an overtly revolutionary one.[10] In other words, anti-expressive rationalism is the flipside of political gradualism. Its superordination of the technical platform to the subject who makes use of or who is abused by it, is the continuation by other means of the traditional social democratic privileging of the speaker's platform to the street action or the picket line. Its political theory is in fact the overconceptualization of an anti-politics in which all processes of transformation through subjective struggle are fastidiously nitpicked into oblivion. This is true even to the extent that its perspective falls somehow staggeringly behind that of the UK civil service bureaucrat who, lately commenting on developments in post-2010 welfare administration, declares that it is the greatest achievement of contemporary state rationality that it has suppressed the "artificial break[s]" between different kinds of marginal political subjects. And it is specifically overconceptualized, rather than simply ideological or mystificatory, because it makes subjective life harder to get a hold of to the measure of its degree of conceptual complexity. The point here is not that the theory should be more plain-talking, but that the plain-talking aversion that the theory transforms is stabilized in that process and not counteracted. In the same way, we often use the category of overcompensation not in order to suggest a degree of compensation that would be more desirable, but rather to show how the energies that are expended in the process of compensation serve to cement more fundamentally into subjective life a tic or symp-

---

10 Its disavowed automatism transforms the traditional vanguardist problem of generals without armies into the newer political problem of superegos in search of metapsychologies. For the same reason, it is the aesthetic and political psychology most appropriate to the topsy-turvy world of a revived radical social democracy in which radical demands are always delivered in a tone of atypical parental reproachfulness.

tom that should not be compensated for at all.[11] In other words, the more intensely and strenuously we defend ourselves, the less energy we have left with which to overcome the circumstances that first inclined us to self-defense. Anti-expressive political rationalists fall behind the perspective of the average civil service bureaucrat because they accept that divisions between people are now unalterable and have to be lived with. In this sense they can be contrasted with another category of person who, according to the terms of anti-expressive rationalism, is unlikely to have any significant influence on their social environment, or, indeed, even to exist. This is the class of expressive political rationalists. By this category I mean to specify, at first in quite vague terms, anyone committed to using modern technical rationality, and in particular the categories and data-forms of bourgeois social knowledge, to extend and enhance their own capacities of moving or insightful political action. Artists who come under this heading are not indifferent to but are obsessed with giving shape to the dynamics of decline, tension, and escalation in subjective political life. They do not fall behind but get ahead of the perspective of modernizing state oppression, by

---

11 The theoretical contribution belongs to Sir Robert Devereux, who in a report on the latest developments of welfare-claimant management asserts that the main benefit of the new technical transformations in British welfare manage is that they "remove that entirely artificial break between being in work and being out of work. Those two things together mean that the conversations that work coaches can now have are quite different from the ones we previously used to have. Previously it was, 'You're out of work; you need to go to work; goodbye.' Now they are working with them continually." When Devereux says that the "breaks" between different categories of person are "artificial," he articulates a basic prejudice of the state itself, according to which any given population ought naturally to present itself as one single continuous and indifferently manageable lump. The force of this prejudice prevents him from recognizing the real state of affairs, which is that making all types of persons equally accessible to state surveillance is itself a work of the highest technological artifice. See Work and Pensions Committee, "Oral Evidence: The Department for Work and Pensions HC 997-I, Wednesday 11 May 2016", https://www.parliament.uk/globalassets/documents/commons-committees/work-and-pensions/160511-DWP.pdf.

expending all of their creative energy in an alternately rancorous and tender effort to give voice to life shut up and reconfigured by advanced clinical and penal procedures. They convert into the principal substance of their work the complex, shifting, and theoretically refractory processes through which hurt life wrenches itself in and out of living immediacy, overleaping the breaks that armchair theorists declare to be insuperable and refusing implacably all forms of technical automatism, both of the quaint Cagean cybernetic variety and its more sophisticated rehabilitation as realistic, overconceptualized indifference to all processes of political self-activity. Finally, they take confidence from the fact that it requires every bit as much draining mental effort to persuade oneself against all the available evidence that the boundaries that inhibit political movement across lines of social division are a priori resistant to any transgression, as it does to undertake the act of transgression itself. The rest of this essay is dedicated to some writing that can be described in these terms. Here is a first approximation to how it might sound:

> I fell back down and rolled over and stared hard at the room and its window, but over the tall swaying grasses my soft mouth, I caressed my long red hair and touched my lips with my lips and a seam from the bottom of my foot to the top of my head began to gently part, releasing a gentle humming silver light, and with a pair of fingers I caught the edge of the light and gently tugged, and it came sliding out, and I held it there in my fingers, I held her there, and I saw my body lying in the grass, and I held the silver light in my hands as her mouth parted, as she lay there in the grass her mouth parted, and with a sigh she breathed in, and the silver light passed into her body, and she lay there, perfect and sated. I have Gender Dysphoria.[12]

---

12 Verity Spott, "Gender Dysphoria," *Two Torn Halves*, March 13, 2016, http://twotornhalves.blogspot.co.uk/2016/03/gender-dysphoria.html. The text is now reprinted in a slightly altered form in Verity Spott, *Trans* Manifestos* (Cambridge: Shit Valley, 2016).

This is the conclusion of a recent poem by the poet and musician Verity Spott. It is only the final passage of the text, which up until this point has proceeded through the narrative coordination of much shorter sentences, some of which consist only of lists of diagnostic data: "I found myself reciting: Melancholia, Asperger's Syndrome, Attention Deficit Hyperactivity Disorder, Gender Dysphoria, Prader Willi's Syndrome, Dyspraxia, Slovenliness, Hayfever, Autistic Spectrum Disorder, Dyslexia & Dyscalculia, Anorexia." The sudden leap outwards into the dizzying paratactic imbrications of this final outcry is prepared for by a counteracting discipline of abbreviation. The flood of assertoric energy in the text I have quoted does not come from nowhere but is stored up through 37 sentences, in each of which the writer is cutting herself off, holding herself back, frustrating the impulse immediately to give voice to the sensations that occasioned the speech-process in the first place, pushing down the desire to cut loose, and so permitting the pressure of frustration to build up incrementally as the text staggers ceaselessly forwards throughout the abstract pathological environment that it constructs. The penultimate sentence preserves and continues this dynamic even as it seems to leave it behind, since its individual coordinating clauses almost without exception could be shut up into independent sentences: "I caressed my long red hair. I touched my lips with my lips." And the fact that they do not do this but instead suddenly open out into one another, reach outside and across themselves and flow into a single expressive current, built up persistently around the single verbal pivot of the coordinating conjunction "and," obeys not a grammatical but rather a psychological imperative. This is the enduring psychological need to break out of the confines of individual subjecthood. The poem is at last ablaze with this need; each of the shorter sentences in the earlier part of the text becomes, in the light of this near conclusion, an allegory of social process, of the fact that it is possible for the whole to move forwards according to a logic that is alien to its constituent parts even when those parts are themselves isolated from one another by social design.

But it is only nearly the conclusion. The actual conclusion of the poem is "I have Gender Dysphoria." Expressionism runs inevitably into its limit of categorical morbidity. The poem works into a new shape Amiri Baraka's dream of a time when

> I will be relaxed.
> When flames and non-specific passion wear themselves
> away. And my eyes and hands and mind can turn
> and soften, and my songs will be softer
> and lightly weight the air.[13]

For Baraka, hurt and exhausting political life — life in "The Party of Insane / Hope" — must hold out the prospect of psychological reprieve in the aftermath of victory. Verity Spott's poem takes hold of that prospect and squeezes from it its excess of Romantic longing. What replaces the horizon of softening is a clinical dead-end: the door to a room that, as Spott says at the beginning of her poem, "I am too afraid to enter." The cheapness of the diagnostic category that might be spoken in that room, which is to say, its definitive stupidity and insignificance, is implicitly contrasted to the actual pain and ecstasy of the experience that it locks down into a medical condition. Everything in Verity's poem leads up to this: each moment in this text is one part of an alternative pathway towards the flat and reified commodity language whose pressure of authority is grounded in the real accumulation of specialized intellectual labor. The real bareness and flat legalism of the final sentence of the text is the flipside of the unbearably overloaded density of the passage that it shuts off. "Gender Dysphoria" is a model lesson in how to relate to that unity: not by parodying the concepts that organize it, or by politely suggesting alternatives to them, but by counterposing

---

13 Amiri Baraka, "Three Modes of History and Culture," in *Transbluesency: The Selected Poems of Amiri Baraka/LeRoi Jones (1961–1995)*, ed. Paul Vangelisti (New York: Marsilio Publishers, 1995), 118.

to them in defiance a whole history of personal and collective endurance.[14]

Whatever this might be said to mean for poetry, one of the things that it more crudely accounts for is the way in which so many contemporary texts present themselves as architectures into which their speaking voices are locked. It accounts for the way in which poets are compelled to write their poems as if they were inescapable penitentiaries, in which delinquent language materials are fenced in by interlocking grates of self-accusation and denial.[15] At its most abstract level this tendency is really only a habit of conception, or a recurrent organizing metaphor; the actual technical effects that it induces, its influence on the syntax and rhythmic pressure and diction of the writer, can only be determined by the way in which they respond to the constraint *after* they have recognized and structured it by means of a visual parallel. In Verity's case the structure becomes a space whose conclusion is a diagnosis locked into place from its beginning, from its title down, as dramatic as a screw in a wall bracket. This is another explanation for the proliferation in the early part of the text of curtailed and confrontationally unpoetic short sentences. "Fell quiet. Saw some figures approaching. Ducked down into the long grass." These are the tentative verbal half-measures of someone who knows that the resolution they've been offered is a trap and who edges towards it as they would towards a precipice, and so the gulps and stutters at the beginning of the text contain in themselves negatively the knowledge that is shouted out in the poem's penultimate sentence. The conclusion that cannot be overcome can only be leapt into with enough vio-

---

14 I am underestimating the complicated gentleness of this poem. But the tender, risible exasperation in which it terminates seems to me as if it can only be achieved by the exaggerated dramatization of the author's impossible effort to outmatch the need for it. Without the maximum polarization of penultimate and final sentence, the defeat temporarily made bearable at the poem's end would not seem tender but only mockingly parodic.

15 "I tried to move but fell right through the eggshells, dropped a floor, lost time, lost weight," Frances Kruk, "lo-fi frags," in *Lo-Fi Frags In-Progress* (London: Veer Books, 2015), 18.

lent impulsiveness that it becomes the cushion of air that we feel beneath us, in free-fall through a syntax disintegrating into its component elements of shock and nervous disorientation. This is where poetry happens, in the maximum polarization of objective conclusion and subjective movement towards it.

One of the things it might be possible to conclude from poetry like Verity Spott's is that the suppression of artificial breaks between the valued and devalued subject induces or encourages a literal suppression of pauses or rests.[16] Could this be the main consequence of the declining costs for capital of access to marginalized personhood, just a new intimacy with the expressive gas pedal? What else might get suppressed in it? What about the artificial break between inside and out, the division which according to anti-expressionist rationalism cannot be revolutionized but only progressively administered? What can be done with the "interior" space in a period in which, more than ever before, that space is positively surfeited with dead technical vocabularies; when, for example, the id refers primarily to "a disorganized (random) brain trajectory" subject to chemical regulation through technical or specialized intervention?[17] In other words, what does it mean that the outgrowth of technical concepts, whose basis is the accumulation of specialized and alienated intellectual labor, is also their grotesque ingrowing?

> out, things
> you that is itself
> the pox, lesion
> fresh piece of motionless
> room you is still sending
> the going is the ceiling is the bulb
> height of annoyance at 1200 watts
> remark the blood & hot

---

16 By this I mean its literal assembly lines: not wage labor altogether.

17 The phrase is from Avi Peled, *NeuroAnalysis: Bridging the Gap between Neuroscience, Psychoanalysis and Psychiatry* (London: Routledge, 2008), 43.

>   out out you Tin of you[18]

Here the scene has changed fundamentally. In these lines by the poet Frances Kruk the architecture of the poem is no longer made up of categories of the bourgeois state upholstered as furniture for a clinical environment. Instead it looks more like an operating theatre, or a skip. Its exit swings open and closed crazily on two- and three-letter hinges. Objects variously broken and gangrenous are thrown into it, they get cursed at and picked over by a voice whose stuttering remissions don't now lead inexorably towards a shattering collision but instead loop round queasily in a circuit, renewing their protest in rhythmic tremors and flinches: aggrieved vocables in a strategy of tension. Repeated sound elements don't get straightforwardly vocalized but are instead dug out like foreign growths. "[O]ut […] lesion […] is […] is […] is […] hot […] out […] out […] you […] Tin […] you." Kruk's poetry is not visibly very much like Spott's, it makes no attempt to hurl itself against intellectual conclusions whose conceptual struts and panels have been fortified by alienated intellectual labor. For the kind of syntactical freefall that you get at the end of "Gender Dysphoria," Kruk's work is simply too preoccupied with its materials, which it picks through with a kind of arch and forensic displeasure, "pull[ing] the guts up through lungs" (131) of administrative speech never before retrenched on by its enabling condition of cakehole. The larger work from which the lines quoted above are taken is a sort of violently collaged treatise on the afterlife of discarded human and material reality. Its "un faced" speaker is confined by genre conventions into a cellar or basement, "from mud to undermud" (112) and dust to underdust, teaching itself with each successive setback and spasm of phonetic arrhythmia new means of multiplying the language resources of those who are pinned viciously to the spot. From time to time it makes a joke out of the revelation of this fact, "back in the basement" (130), "who has heard the basement song & not practiced agony thereafter" (131), but the

---

18   Kruk, "lo-fi frags," 32.

actual language processing of the poetry is deadly serious, or, rather, it is alive to how deadly processing can be, which is to say that it understands the deep affinity between abstract formalism and socially induced mental dissociation very well. Insofar as the poetry takes an interest in anything so tediously general as poetic artifice, it constitutes a practical guide to interiority as meat. Its words and syllables are lodged in one another like bits of food stuck between teeth, dissolved or semi-decomposed even to the level of the grapheme, so that, for example, "hot" in the penultimate line of the passage quoted is "out" with its second letter displaced, turned upside down and distorted. "Out" at the beginning of the passage leads to "in" already swallowed up in "thing," while "in" thus digested is then transferred or excreted into the third line in "lesion," now having itself swallowed up the opening letter of its adversary. The poetry's telescoping of interiority and exteriority, its permanent revolution in grotesque intussusception, has its own music, because the constant necroscopic intrusions into the phonetic interiors of constituent words or living language material produces as its corollary a kind of irritable stuttering, syncopated by the frequency of line breaks and further subdivided by the manic recurrence of dental consonants. The final line ("out out you Tin of you") then merely dramatizes what the poetry is doing *all of the time,* rehearsing in the form of an exasperated joke the chronically purgative disposition at which the writing has already formally arrived, in which expression is not the innocent ventilation of our instincts but instead the laborious, desperate expulsion of the pre-constituted dead labor that mainstream society, and not just mainstream culture, has already assiduously rammed down every throat on which it can get a decent grip.[19] There is no allegory here and no parable. What gets re-done in the final line as narrative is only a phantasmatic backdrop against which a whole voiced alternative to the already alienated interior can be worked out, if not in perfect clarity then in bits and damaged

---

19 The poetry reverts habitually to the same set of worn-out or mass-produced objects: lightbulbs, forks, dust, and used chemicals.

sections, glinting half-visibly through a warped lattice of nerves and gritted teeth.

The music of the most exciting contemporary poetry is defined not by the unprecedented abundance of information that the emancipated poet can access, but instead by the dynamics of an expressionism exercised against the dead labor that has ingrown into the self like a hideous prognosticating nail. In both Verity Spott's and Frances Kruk's writing, living desires and subjective impulses are not separated from a world of alienated labor of which it can only be said that the author is powerless to influence it, but are brought instead under its organized duress from the outset, by means of the established categories of modern clinical practice. Each poet responds differently to this experience of intrusion. In Verity Spott's poem the primary constraint elicits a physiologically concerted effort of expressive outcry, in which the goal is to make a misunion between the conceptually ineliminable diagnosis-conclusion and the explosively torn syntax that leads up to it that is so paradigmatically unbelievable as to make the fact of their present pharisaical unity into a sick and re-energizing joke. In Frances Kruk's it is given the purpose of anatomizing the class content of the idea of surface itself, on which, according to the dominant perspective, abundance is always spread and where the idea that it might be possible to be buried under it is just totally unthinkable.

The two bodies of writing are distinct in their response to the altered historical situation of individual expressive art, and yet each works up into its own intensely singular music of immediate feeling the same basic paradox of advanced capitalist productivity: that where capitalist technique is sufficiently historically advanced, even the most devalued and marginalized lives can flee into their innermost cells and most private desires only to find that it is just here that alienated labor has thrown up its hoarding and is most actively at work. For the anti-expressionist rationalist, this paradox is at root only natural: it is "Our technology / mak[ing] the reVolution for us" on the terrain of subjective existence itself. Inevitably the anti-expressionist's explanation of this state of affairs shades off into a kind of defense. If abstract labor is the hoarding that is built around the ego in the period of its demolition and redevelopment, then anti-expressionist rationalism will be the swathe of decorative slogans pasted up on its cladding, a colorful and gratuitous tribute to the personality forced to queue up outside of itself while objective historical forces tear down its derelict interior. The defense is polemical and it is also conventionally psychoanalytic. Just as it is the basic paradox of capitalist productivity that as technique advances, the official categories used to define marginal (or abject) life become more and more primary repositories of abstract labor, so too is it the basic paradox of institutional-reformist theory that it does not meet intensifications of violent social austerity with a corresponding intensification of subjective resolve, but instead with more and more thoroughgoing attempts preemptively to liquidate personality by means of various overconceptualized forms of impulsive repression — e.g., theories of interpellation.

This is where we end up: Life is the raw material of conceptual paradox and rationalism is the matrix through which it is fed. There are now more conceptual paradoxes in the world than ever before, available in ever more varieties and at ever greater degrees of conceptual sophistication. Whether your preference is for fantasies of technical omnipotence or the deep pathos of atomized despair, some version of anti-subjective rationalism can generate for you the paradoxical sensation you need. To revolutionize this state of affairs, the defenders of these developments counsel a few reformist demands and leave the work of devising expressive slogans to the forces whose most stirring contribution to date is, "Take two three times a day after meals." It is to the great credit of the social actors to whom this kind of slogan is so regularly addressed that they respond by giving a new and impeccably rational meaning to the saying "better out than in."

2

Strong Language:
On Lucy Beynon and Lisa Jeschke

Lucy Beynon and Lisa Jeschke's *David Cameron: A Theatre of Knife Songs* is a half-hour-long play dedicated to the investigation of the question of whether sexual violence against the UK Prime Minister would represent an effective form of political action.[1] It doesn't turn this investigation into a joke, or treat it as a means of demonstrating the obvious truth that politicians, like capitalists, are nothing but character masks for the social relations in which they are caught up. Nor even does it try to make its central premise into a graphic exemplification of a theoretical presupposition, for instance that sexual fantasies of one or

---

1   A video of a performance from June 26, 2014, at the Betsey Trotwood theatre in Clerkenwell, is available on YouTube as Pole Vault, "*David Cameron: A Theatre of Knife-Songs*, Lisa Jeschke & Lucy Beynon, 26 June 2014, Turbamento @ The Betsy Trotwood," *YouTube*, February 9, 2015, https://www.youtube.com/watch?v=1uhG7iOAm0E. A print edition is available as *David Cameron: A Theatre of Knife Songs* (Cambridge: Shit Valley, 2015). All subsequent references to the play are cited parenthetically in text. Two later plays, *The Tragedy of Theresa May* (2017) and *The Decline and Fall of the Home Office* (2019), can also be watched online. See Pole Vault, "THE TRAGEDY OF THERESA MAY," *YouTube*, June 15, 2016, and MayDay Rooms, "The Decline and Fall of the Home Office," *YouTube*, February 15, 2019, https://www.youtube.com/watch?v=djwyIRJ3DWE and https://www.youtube.com/watch?v=YKGUZNtF878.

another kind are possessed of a particular political import or tendency. *David Cameron* is a significant work of art because it shreds and discards all three of these common modes of dealing with personalized and violent fantasies in radical political culture. It shows that all three attitudes are not only insipid or uninspiring because they assume that the representation of the desire for revenge can only ever stand in for something else — the fact of its own ineffectiveness, the real automaticity of capitalist social reproduction, the insurrectionary character of desire in general, etc. — but also because they repress the kind of psychic work needed to take seriously in representation violent impulses or sensations. The play argues that these attitudes not only present a bad account of the relationship between desire and reality, but that they actively connive in the reproduction of the conditions under which no other kind of account could ever be artistically or humanly possible. Their play is a deep investigation into the deadening of the relationship between desire and reality in a liberal culture that is increasingly unreal and was always undesirable. There is nothing else quite like it.

The play is constructed out of several discrete segments, not quite scenes, though any attempt to tell the exact number of these is inhibited by the aggressively shifting tempo of their performance. The most obvious local time-markers are the references to the Thatcher "death parties" that took place in Brixton, Liverpool, and elsewhere in April 2013,[2] but while in the main the dramas of state violence and its projective normalization are shut into a familiarly national idiom, the source materials for the play frequently display a rival influence. The second of the play's "scenes" is an edited recapitulation of the opening section of Büchner's *Woyzeck*, performed in super-sedative slow-motion as if to compensate for lack of sepia tints, while another

---

[2] "When Thatcher died, all the people celebrating at the spontaneous street parties — the media said they were violent. Which they were, because they knew, on a physical, fleshly, cellular level, Margaret Thatcher was, Margaret Thatcher, Prime Minister" (16). E.g., SovietFilms, "MARGARET THATCHER DEAD!! Brixton Celebrates Party — Ghost Town," *YouTube*, April 9, 2013, https://www.youtube.com/watch?v=ikhRGrJReJ8.

deracinates Kleist's *Michael Kohlhaas* from its setting in feudal Saxony in order to resituate it in an anonymous "border control point" — a more intensively policed threshold that could be in Heathrow or the disputed territories of the Ukraine (4). This compounding of English politics and German literary history is self-evidently a conscious decision, and for this it might understandably be accused of being "clever" in the pejorative sense appropriate to public school children and tax avoidance schemes, if only it weren't for the fact that the tone of much of the work is so monumentally crude as to make Barry MacSweeney's disturbing pornographic poems about Margaret Thatcher seem like chaste lyrics of compliment by comparison.[3] The roughness or crudeness of the juxtapositions is itself telling. The stance that the play adopts towards its component materials is both hungry and abrasive. Different types of political or literary material are not included for the purpose of grand displays of erudition but are thrown together hastily by two writers who feel themselves compelled, and who have no wish to conceal the fact that they are compelled, to lay hold of all of the materials to which they have access.

The main contrast in the play is nevertheless not a contrast of literary history, but a contrast of psychological attitudes. The segments themselves often concern the narrative of a professional performer and her unskilled short-term contract dancer, Pawel. Together the two make up a "pop duo," "a small outfit" that is also "just big in a different size" (6), and therefore a kind of diagram of the small-to-medium enterprises that large-to-monopolistic English proprietors have been talking up ever since the UK was still a kind of third-tier absolute monarchy. Within this clinical-entrepreneurial setting, we learn that the

---

3 In MacSweeney's poems from the late 1970s and early '80s the violence of state politics tends to be fully occluded, or perfectly sublimed into the violence wished against the politician Thatcher, with the result that there is left over no reminder of what prompts fantasized violence in the first place. The cycle of part-objects becomes everything. See Barry MacSweeney, *Wolf Tongue: Selected Poems 1965–2000* (Newcastle: Bloodaxe, 2003).

unnamed main character, played by Beynon, "sort of love[s]" David Cameron, though during much of the play she is also engaged in a reflective discussion of whether it would be possible to exact revenge upon him for "his act" by means of "the proper war weapon of rape" (8). Her violent sadism and its autotuned vicissitude into self-annihilating identification is then provided with a counterpoint in Pawel's passive masochism, performed at the play's close by means of a long and disturbing dance sequence that occurs after the singer has quit the stage: a mime routine so preternaturally psychotic that not even Eurovision would be able to stretch itself to accommodate it. Out of the singer's aim-inhibited sadism and Pawel's aimless masochism are drawn the psychic raw materials for a "minor" act that must be made to measure up to the fantasy that David Cameron is larger than the damage he inflicts, and therefore to outrace the predictable conclusion that "his act" will always be able to assign our actions to the merest subplot in a theatre in which he is the impresario.[4]

This constructive view of psychic irresolution is essential to the work. Beynon and Jeschke do not offer to their viewers a catalogue of readymade political ideal types with the order-numbers all ready to be jotted down. Their play forgoes the psychoanalytical account of political desire in which the compound of oedipal love and hatred is destined to be adaptively split off into authoritarian identification and inarticulate rage towards an Other: *Führer* to the left of me, Jew or communist

---

4 For "minor," see Pawel's last word: "Oh, I'm so small. So small and minor. I loved you the whole time, and you didn't even see it. Poor Pawel" (23). For "his act", see the first speech introducing the play's central problem: "Because sometimes I wonder about raping David Cameron. Like, he's such a chunk of embodied violence, could I counter, or match, or punish that violence with the real war weapon of rape … Rape would be such a fully hateful forceful expression of now in the most unresistant, acquiescent way, it makes terrible sense, now, it's reactionary, and even then, even if I raped him back, it still would be so small compared to his act. It's the wrong crime for the job" (8).

or homosexual to the right (or vice versa).[5] And this indecisiveness is important, because it would at least have been possible to write a play in which the main lesson was that, ultimately, the politics of revenge against the contemporary symbol of oppression reverses inevitably into a docile love relation. *David Cameron* does in fact contain this conclusion, but since the conclusion does not come last or get invested with the character of a sensible summing up, it merely ends up seeming like an afterthought or offshoot, a byproduct of the work thrown off into an incidental punchline: "So to conclude, I don't think raping David Cameron would work. Besides, I sort of love him." This thought arrives on page 10 of a text 23 pages in length and is of course no conclusion at all. All it does is terminate one sequence of the play, which then veers off into a long skit about work — itself an unstable compound in which *working through* is forever liable to be frozen into "a job well done," one of the one hundred and eleven things that Beynon declares that she "loves" on pages eleven and twelve, in a great list of dubious love objects crammed together like inmates shoehorned into an overnight cell. Probably the psychological category that would be best suited to describe all of this is ambivalence; but what Beynon and Jeschke do with this category needs to be specified quite carefully. The two characters at the center of *David Cameron* are split-off halves of a single integral unit like the two characters at the center of Brecht's *Seven Deadly Sins of the Petty Bourgeoisie*, and each proves to be ambivalent in turn in the mode of expres-

---

5   This is the pattern developed in, for example, Wilhelm Reich's *Mass Psychology of Fascism*, though Reich's conception of upstanding genital health inclines him to emphasize passive submission to a *Führer* over active hatred for an outsider or other as the principle characteristic of fascist psychology, see Wilhelm Reich, *The Mass Psychology of Fascism*, trans. Mary Boyd Higgins (Harmondsworth: Penguin, 1970). The opposite emphasis is given in Adorno and Horkheimer's chapter on anti-Semitism in *The Dialectic of Enlightenment*, trans. John Cumming (London: Verso, 1979), where experiences of subordination are always merely preludes to intense desires for revenge: "the hatred of the led [...] knows no bounds" (171).

sion that he or she adopts.⁶ This judgment would imply a particular focus of argument. Ambivalence is a state convenient for inducing social quiescence, because, as Wilhelm Reich already recognized the better part of a century ago, and as has been repeated by psychoanalysts of all tendencies ever since, "to be non-political [or to be positively undecided] is not, as one might suppose, evidence of a passive psychic condition, but of a highly active attitude."⁷ Beynon and Jeschke's play might be thought to evince a basic solidarity with this idea, that states of apparently placid indecision are wasteful or exhausting, but their argument is also more complex than this, because it maintains that the attempt to deny ambivalence, as well as to maintain oneself in it, is itself intensely exhausting and subjectively destructive. The play *David Cameron* recognizes two species of such denial: first, the attempt to imagine that we can harness feelings of intense hatred in order to achieve our political goals without suffering the experience of vicissitude or reversal; and second, and more important, the idea that by recognizing the reproduction of ambivalence in the effort to fabricate a sensation adequate to the situation in which we find ourselves, the way is open to us to reconceive radical politics and its relationship to art without our needing to consume ourselves in a vain effort of self-fashioning. This second idea is also a denial of ambivalence, although it appears to be based on a more intelligently conscious recognition of it. It sees that in the effort to make ourselves entertain a particular feeling or desire, we do nothing but establish the conditions in which the opposite feeling can come to expression; and it repudiates this violent struggle with the self as a reproduction of ambivalent psychic attitudes at a higher order of intensity. For the sophisticated denier of the wasteful logic of psychologi-

---

6 *The Seven Deadly Sins of the Petty Bourgeoisie* is one of a number of Brecht plays in which two characters represent two distinct "sides" of, or possibilities for, a single person. Other examples are *The Yes-Sayer*, *The No-Sayer*, and *The Good Person of Szechwan*. See Bertold Brecht, "The Seven Deadly Sins", in *Collected Plays, Volume 2*, eds. John Willett and Ralph Manheim (London: Methuen Drama, 1994).

7 Reich, *The Mass Psychology of Fascism*, 233. Brackets added by the author.

cal ambivalence, the first step to the restoration of lost psychological energies is the recognition of the fact that ambivalence cannot be fought against by means of the attempt to identify ourselves with some extreme attitude or feeling. Its promoters ask, what is to be gained by forcing ourselves into mental situations where we suffer the feelings we wish to oppose more and not less acutely? How could the struggle against one's basic psychological tendencies ever be more than an elaborate species of self-harm?

In answering these questions, Beynon and Jeschke argue that the attempt to harness strong desire *is* vain, self-destructive, and formidably counterproductive, *and that it is still worth undertaking*—that the conscious recognition of ambivalence does not free up psychological energy but only wastes it differently. The adoption of this position is one of the play's great risks. It is also its main challenge to a culture of people who it genuinely and vibrantly loathes, who find in their own equanimity an exit from wasted energies shaped like the utility-maximizing grownups that they believe themselves to have become. These people tell themselves that they have been liberated from the belief that they need to *make themselves* feel something, by the reassuring analytical precept that says that this labor of self-production or self-manipulation is something that is only done by people who are trying unsuccessfully to fend off an impulse of an equal and opposite tendency. Beynon and Jeschke's rejection of this thinking is a risk because it is perverse and cannot be proven — we cannot prove that those who see in the effort to fabricate adequate sensation merely a heightening of ambivalence and an intensification of unproductive internal conflict are themselves the most damaged and self-wasting subjects of all. Nor can we prove that the injunction to desist in forcing subjective attitudes is more akin to the psychotic fantasy of violent revenge than the performance that strains actually to inhabit that fantasy and therefore to impel us to contemplate it as a real possibility, rather than as a joke or provocation. The play exposes this attempt to escape from ambivalence as a false inference from the correct recognition that all efforts to fight against subjective uncertainty raise ambivalence to a higher level of intensity. It constructs out of the vicissitudes to which it exposes itself the rudiments or outlines of a consciously transformative political language.[8]

This language is naturally energetic. Everywhere in the play-text internal conflict is permitted to run riot in the involutions of a basic conversational syntax. From the very first passage in which the rape of David Cameron is tabled and then withdrawn, Beynon's grammar decomposes into a particle-storm of competing time-markers: "Rape would be such a fully hateful forceful expression of now in the most unresistant, acquiescent way, it makes terrible sense, now, it's reactionary, and even then, even if I raped him back, it would still be so small compared to his act" (8). Rape as a fantasy of revenge for inflicted social damage is an expression of "now," a condensation of its salient features as expressive as flared jeans for the 1970s. The hypotactic run-on clause that proceeds from this gross metonymy inserts the same word but trusses it up in commas, *now,* as if by way of emphasis, refuting preemptively the still unarticulated objection that it was just as bad then or else that things aren't going to get better any time soon, only then for the thought to wander off in just the direction that it had seemed definitely to prohibit, veering into the adverbial phrase "even then" as if in flight from its own basic instincts. "[E]ven then" would indicate a qualifying circumstance ("even in this situation") rather than a time reference, but no anterior qualifying circumstance has been specified, which is why the speaker is forced to clarify by adding another phrase, "even if I raped him back," a gloss that does not diminish but instead reinforces the temporal sense (the

---

8   The distinctions in the preceding two paragraphs are perhaps hair splitting and are certainly inadequate to their object. But the same point could just as easily be made by describing the experience of reading good poetry. The aesthetics that attempts to deny ambivalence is based on the false assumption that our true desires are desires that we can have sustainably all the time; but this is a stupid lie whose intellectual basis is the conflation of desires with subjective constants like skills, experiences, certification, and other objects that are capable of being anatomized into bullet points on the cover letter of a CV.

presence of the past) precisely because it seems anxiously calculated to deny it or otherwise ward it off.

None of the untidiness of this apostrophe is incidental to what is being said or divisible from the progress of its argument. In the first instance this is because disputes about what is politically singular about the present moment are always accompanied by the anxiety that our claims to novelty are deluded. In the second, it is because what is being proposed by Beynon and Jeschke is based on the paradoxical idea that the novelty of our current political situation is defined by its potential for violent psychological regression. Logical argument in the passage slides back into temporal description because of the play's more encompassing practical commitment, to the truth that what we want for ourselves now cannot in any circumstances be disaggregated from who we are. And at the bottom of this reversal is a problem to do with the meaning of confidence. If our "act" is "so small," as Beynon's character admits that it would have to be *even if* it were to outline an intervention of the most "hateful" or "forceful" violence, is this because according to some felicific calculus it is always eclipsed by the costs of never-ending fiscal austerity? Or is it because the confidence that the act is capable of artificing, the anger that it brings to expression, and the violence that it articulates, are all ultimately available only to people who have elected to regress into a realm of fantasy — a private theater in which the active performer (Beynon) and the passive one (Jeschke) are never anything more than stock characters? What kind of act could make the performance of confidence something more than a conscious display?

The idea that extreme acts in art are "small" because they are imaginative and not real is part of what today passes for cultural common sense. It is the main instrument through which forms of psychological self-harm are transformed into a model of aesthetic experience. In March 2015, the novelist Marina Warner, Dame Commander of the Order of the British Empire, restated some of these positions in the *London Review of Books* in an article titled "Learning My Lesson."[9] The text, which is mainly given over to detailing measurement practices in UK higher education institutions, and which was occasioned by Warner's resignation from the University of Essex, reminds us that fiction "gives you permission" to do what you ought not to do, and is thus essential to the process through which flexible and tolerant citizens are nurtured into poll booths and civil society organizations. Warner recalls in this connection the improving advice she once gave to a "young Emirati Arab" in her creative writing class: "[I]t isn't you speaking but someone whose voice you are making up as you write, so you are free — or rather you can be more free there, in that space of imagination — to think around things, exploring possibilities." This will seem, and in fact also is, a quite standard representation of the autonomy of the imagination and the different order of moral values to which it ought to be held to account. It is the vision of the freedom of the mind, or of the artistic imagination, that has been common to liberal writers seeking an accommodation with constituted power ever since Coleridge disavowed his early calls for regicide, on the basis that he was "merely" imagining them. Most of us who think of this position in Warner's article as an idle and politically noxious cliché will feel our eyes glazing over before we reach the next sentence. But it is worth pausing here, since her patrician benevolence is also possessed of its own internal economy of psychological energies, and because this is exactly the type of attitude that I think that Beynon and Jeschke are working to bring into view. The freedom of the imagination, which is based on an abjection of personality, or on the disowning of the desires that are imputed to a character, does not open up a space of total license, but only makes us, more cautiously, "more free," incrementally less unfree than we might be in the authoritarian UAE or its near anagram the University of Essex. Why Warner thinks this qualification is significant is not easy to say. It could

---

9   Marina Warner, "Learning My Lesson," *London Review of Books* 37, no. 6 (March 19, 2015), https://www.lrb.co.uk/the-paper/v37/n06/marina-warner/learning-my-lesson.

be because she is aware that the idea of the total freedom of the imagination is a useless romantic fantasy; or because she wants to invest the idea with some atmosphere of psychological plausibility; or because she thinks, in the best tradition of liberal colonialism, that total freedom is something for which "young Emirati Arab" women aren't yet prepared. Perhaps all of these possibilities mount up to the same thing. Nevertheless, the ambiguity of the diagnosis maintains its own independent value. Warner doesn't say why the freedom of the imagination should be qualified or circumscribed, and the ultimate significance of this omission is that the circumscription comes to appear as if it were, or at least as if it could be, self-evidently justifiable. There is no reason to ask why we need to be "more free" and not free altogether, because the readership to whom Warner addresses her plea for Western liberal values has already performed the psychic work necessary to accept that the separation of imagination and action is inert and anyway not worth fighting against. It is the fundamental accomplishment of the culture in whose defense articles like "Learning My Lesson" are written that the lessening of subjective intensity implicit in the idea that the imagination is at once split off *and* recuperable, "more free" *and* constrained, appears as a description of how things naturally are and not as the result of a process of repressive self-enfeeblement.

The pseudo-drama of the liberation of the "Arab" in our liberal university system is important to this conception, but the more fundamental reason why the effort of mental conception has no place in this idea of the imagination is that the repression of effort is the aim that it labors most strenuously to accomplish. Anyone who tries to make herself feel something she doesn't want, or to want something she doesn't feel, is from this perspective engaged not in making art but in a sort of perverse self-degradation. And this is itself reminiscent of other forms of what to a Warnerian eye seem like morally compromising forms of labor, like that of the women who allow themselves to be employed in the coke heaps of South Wales in the 1860s:

> I love female night shift workers. They quote quote are exposed to the deterioration of character, arising from their loss of self-respect unquote unquote. Strength of language varies directly with deterioration of character in that as one's bodily commitment increases, as you spend more blood on keeping someone else's private pension wet with it, the language which is summoned to stem and then counter that blood loss must strengthen.[10]

This quotation of a quotation in Marx belongs to the most intense passage of *David Cameron* and to the segment in which the problems of liberal auto-constraint are addressed with the most focused and explicit energy.[11] The inverse correlation that

---

10 Beynon and Jeschke, *David Cameron*, 13. The rest of the segment runs: "[…] When this organised country rips your heart out of your chest and uses it to supplement his own beating campaign for flesh, THEN WHAT IS AN OBJECTION TO STRONG LANGUAGE? In the face of that act Fuck the man that does that. Fuck him not with the tenderness of parodic loving sex play, but fuck him like they say Dworkin thought every fuck fucked. Fuck him in the face that soft-powered poverty into itself. Fuck him in the hands that write the speeches, fuck him in the fleshless mouth that speaks them. Rip him a cunt of his own invention and let him see how that compares to a cunt of human flesh, loudly throbbing. Fuck his gash. It's nothing like mine. He has sorely misunderstood. And to call for calm, for gentler terms, is cultural Cameron."

11 The quote is from the Fourth Report of the Children's Employment Commission, given in a footnote in *Capital, Volume I*, in Marx and Engels, *Collected Works of Marx and Engels*, 50 vols. (London: Lawrence & Wishart, 1975–2004), 35:264: "Both in Staffordshire and in South Wales young girls and women are employed on the pit banks and on the coke heaps, not only by day but also by night. This practice has been often noticed in Reports presented to Parliament, as being attended with great and notorious evils. These females employed with the men, hardly distinguishable from them in their dress, and begrimed with dirt and smoke, are exposed to the deterioration of character, arising from the loss of self-respect, which can hardly fail to follow from their unfeminine occupations." This argument prompts anger because it affects to speak about "deterioration" in the labor process as if it were a purely moral phenomenon, but the reason I think it is interesting to Beynon and Jeschke is that its transgression of a common sense distinction ("deterioration" is a strictly physical fact) at once mirrors and reduces to a kind of joke the same kind of transgression as the one

it sets up between "[s]trength of language" and "deterioration of character" does not just assert a relationship between language or the kinds of fantasies we express with it and anything so gruesome and abstract an object of academic dissertations as "the Body." Instead, it argues that the effort to expose the imagined desires that we are compelled to have, rather than the ones we are encouraged to consume, and to live with them, is the first step in freeing ourselves from the state of habitualized ambivalence in which we unconsciously waste and discard our energies up to the point where it seems as if we are by nature perfectly serene. The prefabricated identity of "strong language" and "bad language" arises naturally out of this scene of repressive injunctions like methane from manure. It is a form of the moral code that is used to tell certain kinds of people that it is bad for them to be strong, both in the diagnostic sense that it leads to pathologies and in the theocratic sense that says that they ought to remain in their place. To make "bodily commitment" "stem and then counter" the loss of blood and desire and life that is prerequisite to and not excluded by the conscious experience of serenity means not only *to work* but also to acknowledge the effects of the work that we have already been made to do. Beynon and Jeschke's point is not the simplistic and common one that actual social misery is in the end "worse than" bad language, so that those who castigate bad language are cultivators of indifference to actual "bodily" or social human suffering; this idea, which has been done to death by serene theoreticians who know absolutely nothing about what it means to fight to stay alive, is really not so different from the conception of the mind threnodized by such liberal imperialists as the novelist Marina Warner. Beynon and Jeschke's point is rather that the fight for sensations that are strong and weak at once, compassionate and aggressive, cannot occur without a struggle that not only opens us to damage but which actively threatens to induce it. "Deterioration" is not only

---

they themselves are determined to carry out, against the idea that art must in the end have absolutely nothing in common with real experiences of exhaustion or suffering.

historical; the labor that is necessary actually to face the fact of it requires of us that we accept its extension in ourselves. Only in a concerted effort to make our desires and our actions bend towards one another is it possible to imagine a situation where the fucking economics textbook with its fixed and predictable relationships might blur or flame up into the medical manual in which blood loss can not only be "stem[med]" but also "counter[ed]," where blood can also flow back into the body, not in inverse correlation to anything but in defiance of all relationships that we have ever been taught to know.

When Beynon and Jeschke write, and when Beynon yells, "THEN WHAT IS AN OBJECTION TO STRONG LANGUAGE?" (13), the assertion does not mean (although by anyone who is not listening it may always be read to mean) that we should resist the moral imperative of proportionality that is always asserted by those whose own actions exceed any scale of ordinary moral language. What it really means, which is to say, what it means more intensely and uniquely, is that it is only when language itself becomes exhausting, and not merely a reflection on exhaustion or a complaint about our orders of priority, that it can really begin to articulate just how much human life is wasted in a world in which the pathology that forces people to acquiesce to their smallness is forever being imposed upon the idea of culture itself. In March 2015, in the dreary runup to another general election, in which state politicians will talk indefatigably about how much we need to save for the future, Beynon and Jeschke's play reminds us that our most significant acts do not occur periodically according to a calendar determined at the convenience of our ruling classes, but fitfully and beautifully and counter to our best habits and educated expectations. They cannot happen over and over again forever, because they require of us an expenditure of life and instinct that is frightening and painful and sometimes damaging to undergo. The great accomplishment of the "small act" *David Cameron* throughout all of its vicissitudes and inevitable reverses is that it makes the real inevitability of large collective acts of this kind feel undoubtable in a period in which the pressure to doubt them is ferocious and hatefully ubiquitous and unabating.

3

Class Separation vs. Separation Anxiety: A Brief Psychotic Interlude

In the third chapter of his *Reflections On Violence,* "Prejudices Against Violence," the French revolutionary syndicalist and soon-to-be monarchist Georges Sorel explained why it was necessary for the proletariat to retain a strict separation from the middle class. "Everything may be saved," Sorel wrote,

> if the proletariat, by their use of violence, manage to reestablish the division into classes, and so restore to the middle class something of its former energy; that is the great aim towards which the whole thought of men — who are not hypnotised by the events of today, but who think of the condition of tomorrow — must be directed.[1]

The condition of salvation that is imagined here exists in the grand tradition of modern regenerative brutality stretching from Walter Raleigh to his insurgent antipode Frantz Fanon. Violence is at first conceived in it as the political equivalent of a sudden awakening. In Fanon's language, it retrieves its agent

---

1   Georges Sorel, *Reflections on Violence,* ed. Jeremy Jennings (Cambridge: Cambridge University Press, 1999), 85.

from a state of "aboulia," or absence of willpower,[2] transfiguring those "who are inert, cannot make plans, who have no resources [and] who live from day to day" into the bearers of "a national destiny and a collective history."[3] In the language of Sorel, it wrenches its agent out of a state of "hypnosis" and fixes his attention upon the great mythical display cabinet of tomorrow, as well as its trophy-"condition."

For anyone who now passes their days isolated "trying to defeat or gratify powerful impulses in a world [they] fear," this "condition" may feel unreal even before they begin to consider whether or not it may be desirable.[4] The politics of regressive separation — "taking back control", "our" borders, "legitimate concerns", etc. — are more alive now than they have been at any time in the last fifty years; and the psychological para-politics of fear and aversiveness are revived with them simultaneously and to a still greater degree. Furthermore, as this revival picks up speed across multiple election cycles and throughout the whole atmosphere of so-called public opinion, the process throws up its own sub-tendency, in the form of a newly urgent, reactive politics of compulsory and defensive unity. This is the tedious liberal catchall complaint about political "divisiveness." What could radical separateness in Sorel's sense even mean in these circumstances — if indeed there ever was such a thing, and the theory of class separation for which he became known was ever anything but a kind of elaborate justification for ascetic puritanism, with all of the tendencies towards sexual suffocation and displaced misogyny that flourish at its root?

The following chapter tries to answer this question. It is not a history of the political-economic changes that have given rise to regressive separation, or that have made earlier politics of class separation wither away, but it is instead a brief and provisional attempt to explain one psychological relationship between fas-

---

2 Frantz Fanon, *The Wretched of the Earth,* trans. Constance Farrington (London: Penguin 1961), 228.
3 Ibid., 73.
4 Richard Wright, *Native Son* (London: Vintage, 2000), 73.

cist demands for racial or ethnic segregation and liberal demands for national unity, and to show how in both worldviews the fraught and painful fact of separation is harmfully denied and precluded from meaningful expression. For the same reason, it is one element of a broader account of the instinct for separation in a militant and transformative culture.

•

On June 16, 2016, six days before the referendum on UK EU membership, the British neo-Nazi Thomas Mair murdered the Labour MP and "Remain" supporter Jo Cox. The killing was a testimony to the historical and psychoanalytic significance of the need for separation over unity. Mair was reported to be a "loner" with strong symptoms of depression and compulsion neurosis.[5] In the days after Cox's death, the newspapers that reported pruriently on his habits of obsessive self-cleaning also noted his search record on the computers at the library outside which he would later shoot and stab Cox. This included queries about matricide,[6] a desire that was linked in Mair's mind with the relationship his mother had formed with a British Caribbean man during his middle adolescence.[7] The violence through

---

[5] BBC News, "Thomas Mair: Extremist loner who targeted Jo Cox," *BBC*, November 23, 2016, http://www.bbc.co.uk/news/uk-38071894.

[6] Hatred of mothers is a consistent preoccupation of personality types that incline towards movement fascism (i.e., rabid fascist extremists), as Klaus Theweleit and Christina Wieland have shown in their writings on the institutions of masculinity. See Klaus Theweleit, "Männliche Geburtsweisen," in *Das Land das Ausland heist: Essays, Reden, Interviews zu Politik und Kunst* (Munich: Deutscher Taschenbuch Verlag, 1995), and Christina Wieland, *The Undead Mother: Psychoanalytic Explorations of Masculinity, Femininity, and Matricide* (London: Karnac, 2000).

[7] Richard Spillett, "'Jekyll and Hyde' assassin was a loner who scoured himself with Brillo pads because of cleanliness obsession and spent his life on mental health drugs," *Daily Mail*, November 23, 2016, http://www.dailymail.co.uk/news/article-3960988/Jekyll-Hyde-Jo-Cox-assassin-Thomas-Mair.html. In the *Mail* article, Mair's half-brother Duane St Louis is quoted as saying that "[h]e has never expressed any views about Britain, or shown any racist tendencies. I'm mixed race and I'm his half-brother, we got on

which he hoped, in Sorelian terms, "to manage to reestablish [...] division" played out in the key of fantasized restitution, recalling such other rifts between overt purpose and deed in the vocabulary of the US extreme right as conversion therapy and corrective rape. Its unconscious attempt to transform a passive, infantile fear of abandonment or extreme separation anxiety into an active, grown-up desire to enforce a regime of ethnic apartheid,[8] is only the latest historical expression of the repressive attitude that Sorel would pompously celebrate as the "resigned abnegation of men who strive uncomplainingly."[9]

---

well. He never married. The only time I remember him having a girlfriend was as a young man, but a mate stole her off him. He said that put him off [women] for life." This is of course just a decontextualized pull quote, and in its original usage it was intended primarily to indicate that Mair's act was not ideological but only disturbed, in accordance with the desire of the *Mail* and the majority of the British news media to disassociate the murder from the general atmosphere of the campaign for the "Leave" vote, for which the *Mail* and the majority of the British news media was of course directly, and perhaps primarily, responsible. But it does seem at least to suggest the centrality to Mair's fantasy life of some primal rage at perceived abandonment, that his first experience of desertion by a partner should be treated as if it were an irreparable and inexpiable wrong, for which all women in general are to be indifferently held responsible. The idea that it "put [Mair] off for life" is one indication that he had in fact already been put off, and that his first adult experience of relationship trouble was seized upon as an opportunity to rationalize, and so to take possession of, what would otherwise have remained a merely troubling and inexplicable aversion. Likewise, it is conspicuous in Duane St Louis's account that the man who "stole" Mair's girlfriend brought about no lasting transformation in Mair's general attitude towards "mates." The selective apportionment of blame conforms to a familiar pattern. If the child suffers, it must be the fault of the mother, never of the father: always the EU, never the member state.

8 The thought process evidences a conventional inversion: Mair believed that his mother deserved to die because she was a "race traitor": white supremacism serves to rationalize a preexisting desire and therefore to give to it a semblance of meaning. It might be wondered whether this helps to explain why Mair's desire to kill his mother, although conscious, was also inactive, so that newspapers could report that he had spent the day before the murder re-tuning his mother's TV. Cox was of course the ultimate victim of these displacements.

9 Sorel, *Reflections on Violence*, 228.

It is necessary to talk about Cox's murder like this, in spite of the dangers of pathological readings of fascism, and in spite of the risks of converting hateful political assassination into a portfolio of materials for an amateur case study, because it is important to keep in view, at the root of racist divisiveness, some wildly distorted demand for unity. Murder in the name of fascist violence originates in a convulsively distorted protest against the conditions that it reproduces. This principle of interpretation is valuable, not because it helps us to remember that ultimately fascists are hurt and complex human beings, full of inarticulate anguish and perhaps also one day subject to rehabilitation,[10] but because it helps us to see how gestures of premature reconciliation in the name of the divided national community are not necessarily the opposite of feverish moralizing about the virtue of violent segregation, but are just as frequently the elaborations of an identical process of self-therapy, only now uttered in a language of more refined purpose and with a greater consistency of form and expressive content.[11] It is today January 21, 2017. It

---

10 Although patently it won't be Thomas Mair or even the members of a fucking Nazi gang like National Action who will benefit most significantly from the conversion of the United Kingdom into an outsized tax-free headquarters, which in the absence of any other means of commanding a share of total global surplus value is what its asset-holding political class now intends to make of it.

11 To drag slightly out of context a line of Leo Bersani's: "[B]rutality is identical to [...] idealization": *Is the Rectum a Grave? And Other Essays* (Chicago: University of Chicago Press, 2009), 29. Incidentally, if Bersani is right in his thesis, and what is stereotypically treated as "passive" sexuality (i.e., in male heterosexual assumptions concerning gay sex and female sexuality) is identified with, and organically repeats, a pleasure that is felt during episodes of infancy in which the child is faced with the loss of identity, then it makes sense that a person who experienced special pain due to helplessness or abandonment during a later stage in childhood might eventually turn against this earlier sense of loss of control with a special intensity, and condemn its perceived corollaries in adult sexual life with an aggressive aversiveness that seems pathetically overblown even when viewed in comparison to the "ordinary" prejudices of the dominant (i.e., male heterosexual) social outlook (*Is the Rectum a Grave?*, 24). The relationship between these two perspectives is apologetically summarized by the brother of Mair's inspiration David Copeland, in an episode of the

is more than seven months since Cox's murder. Yesterday Donald Trump was inaugurated as president of the United States, talking in the language of a Hollywood scriptwriter about the necessity of confronting "American carnage." The liberal-parliamentarian press disgorges an unending series of condemnations of divisiveness, appeals for healing, pious wishes for the re-creation of a non-existent unity. It tacitly acknowledges the impotence of these declarations by projecting its own internal anxiety onto the outgoing President Obama, or else onto "his wife," substituting for active resistance to authoritarian state populism a comforting fantasy of paternal invulnerability, the tweediness of which is so blazingly and absolutely out of sync with reality as to seem actually laughable:

> Obama descended the steps shoulder to shoulder with Trump, chatting and sharing a joke. At the bottom, Obama smiled broadly. His wife could not hide an expression akin to melancholy. He lifted her hand to his lips and kissed it, giving her a reassuring smile.[12]

Here, and in passages that are akin it, the liberal and humane call for unity and healing — Obama and Trump, shoulder to shoulder! — exhibits by virtue of its precipitousness just that kind of false resolution that in the psychohistory of a neo-Nazi transforms fear and despair at the prospect of separation into a catastrophic political need for it. It is a model example of what

---

BBC's *Panorama* series aired in 1999: "I think he [David Copeland] just had a healthy dislike of gays, like most of the male gender have, not a hatred, just a dislike." Copeland was convicted in 1999 for a series of bombings aimed at ethnic minorities and what he enviously understood to be the London gay "community." Mair ordered his first consignment of weapon assembly manuals ten days after Copeland's first court appearance. See BBC, *Panorama: "The Nailbomber,"* June 30, 2000, http://news.bbc.co.uk/hi/english/static/audio_video/programmes/panorama/transcripts/transcript_30_06_00.txt.

12 Joanna Walters, "Obama Departs White House with a Promise: 'I'll be right there with you,'" *The Guardian,* January 20, 2017, https://www.theguardian.com/us-news/2017/jan/20/barack-obama-departs-white-house.

Freud called "the splitting of the ego in the process of defence."[13] Everywhere I look this kind of false resolution seems to reproduce itself, in every byway and backroad of political discourse. It recurs wherever some true political aspiration is made too quickly into the basis for reassuring political generalization.

Of course liberals will not all endorse Trump explicitly, even if they continue to defend political measures that in the long run will help right-wing nationalism to thrive; and in fact many will despise him with the peculiar, heightened intensity of those who feel themselves to have been placed under threat for the very first time. But the argument that I am making is not that liberalism is incapable of endorsing separation or antagonism under any circumstances, but that in general it misconceives of the way in which the need for separation is originated and resolved. It needs to do this. Within the worldview implied by the average editorial in the *New York Times,* aversion to any analysis of the psychological need for unity is what permits the reproduction of unity as a political demand. It is only by means of this mechanism that liberal thinking can free itself from the recognition that in this class society, the abstract attempt to effect reconciliation is just as likely to express itself in acts of reactionary violence as it is in the emergence of new relations of mutual support. Put more directly, liberal thinking is averse to the psychological need for unity because that need arises not only in the face of threats to those liberal privileges that are embodied in the constitutional bourgeois state, but also in the face of deepening poverty, disintegrating family structures, under-employment or super-exploitation, landlordism, benefit cuts, news of distant family uprooted by bombs and foreign-armed militia, and above all in the deep personal recognition of exclusion that is the main element of class culture in a society no longer premised on formal segregation. Its desire to limit discussion of unity strictly to the domain of politics is therefore paradoxically its

---

13 Sigmund Freud, "The Splitting of the Ego in the Process of Defence," in *Complete Psychological Works of Sigmund Freud,* Vol. 23, ed. James Strachey et al. (London: Vintage, 2001), 275–79.

main method for obfuscating the historical expression of class experience as such, and thus of disclaiming its own participation in the reactionary violence against which it believes itself to be the single, indispensable bulwark.[14]

Where does this leave us? The amateur enthusiast of neo-Nazism attempts to manage real individual trauma by transplanting it into a political fantasy of ethnic-national self-defense, while, by contrast, the professional advocate of unity under the auspices of liberal democracy deals with trauma by means of wish fulfilment — the dream of us all standing together "shoulder to shoulder." Georges Sorel could not have foreseen the deep integrity of this state of affairs any more than could Marx or Rosa Luxemburg. But what does it mean that in both social outlooks the fact of separation or exclusion remains studiously denied or suppressed? If the desire to remain abstemiously separate from any culture in particular has now become decisively reactionary, while the political demand for unity continues under present conditions to be lifelessly premature, how can the experience of separation be radicalized?

Transformative political art has to recognize, and wherever it already exists it does recognize in practice, that the history of class separation is in reality the history of capitalist unification. It is the gigantic expansion and integration of capitalist exploitation across the world and its implacable forced entry into every domain and level of human experience that determines the false resolution of Sorel's mythical vision into the pseudo-world history of Thomas Mair, abreacting from the comfort of his computer his unconscious rage at abandonment, and transforming it into the conscious wish fulfillment of small town NSDAP-revivalism. And there is now no country and constituency or

---

[14] It follows from this that the criterion for a progressive politics of unity is that a movement should always articulate its response to the immediate, defensive demands of the situation in a practical vocabulary that is adequate to the experience of the excluded — who are emphatically not only from "the white working class" — in disregard of the interests of those who have never previously been excluded from anything and who would now gladly place themselves at the head of the "anti-fascist" resistance.

region where a Sorelian politics of "class separation" can bring about any more desirable result, since even the most extravagant nationalist pageantry and the wildest impostures about "historic movement[s]"[15] are incapable of disguising the fact that beneath the blizzards of confetti, no more significant qualitative transformation has taken place then the dignified metamorphosis of Thomas Mair's public computer into the voting booth of every enfranchised adult citizen.

What Sorel thought of as the "energy" of working-class culture is now produced not in abstemious withdrawal from bourgeois values and institutions, but in the hungry and confrontational seizure of means and instruments and modes of expression from which the working class has historically been excluded. That is to say, it belongs in the intense and historically legitimate need for bourgeois privilege, backed up by a knowledge of the fundamental role of aggression in overcoming the forces that prohibit access to it. You can see this in all working-class youth cultures now available via YouTube and in the activity of working-class performers of all ages and genders. The wild psychotherapy of their culture does not culminate in fascist identitarianism or its practical endorsement under the inert heading of a National Healing Process, but in unity-through-seizure, movement for the sake of it, property violation, the experimental crossing of defined boundaries, self-dissipation, the rage of passivity, etc., all lived out throughout and against the incessant integration of global capital and the speech-acts of its many left- and right-wing advocates.

Could there be in our world now any residual significance in the idea that the task of anti-capitalist artists is to create a separate and independent worldview, sectioned off from bourgeois reality not by a wall or by a checkpoint, but by an energy that is so clearly its own that middle-class consumers would

---

[15] "Everyone is listening to you now. You came by the tens of millions to become part of a historic movement, the likes of which the world has never seen before": Time Staff, "Read Donald Trump's Full Inauguration Speech," *Time,* January 20, 2017, updated January 24, 2017, http://time.com/4640707/donald-trump-inauguration-speech-transcript/.

instinctively flinch from it? The radical theory that answers this question by declaring that separation is already over and done with, because capital now "surpasses the division between employment and unemployment, working and non-working, productive and assisted, precarious and non-precarious" — all of the "divisions on which the left has based its categories of thought and action" — and that concludes that anti-capitalists "must rise to [the same] level of abstraction [...] if we want to avoid being swept away" — this theory is in fact only half right.[16] It's right, because the raw fact of historical development does in truth point towards the overcoming of working-class separation both as a reality and as an aspiration. But it's wrong, too, because it is only in the lexicon of banal received ideas that separation is always simply beneath consideration and abstraction is something to which we invariably rise up. The conclusions are just too tediously familiar. For a more confrontational class culture, in which the threat of exclusion masses in the sky above our heads, and abstraction just as frequently advertises its openings beneath our feet, they represent a glaring reality deficit. And it would be more true to say that in a world whose complete integration is more liable to abstract assertion than it has ever been, what radical culture needs to separate itself from is not the history of bourgeois values (whatever they are) but the enormous, narcissistic complacency of those who profess to believe in their universal availability.

It is because even the most progressive middle-class appeals for unity totally lack this instinctive recognition, that they share at some deep and mostly unconscious level an uncomfortable affinity with the murderous demands for segregation of the fascists whom we are supposed to unite against.

---

16 This quote is from Maurizio Lazzarato, *The Making of the Indebted Man: An Essay on the Neoliberal Condition,* trans. Joshua David Jordan (Los Angeles: Semiotext(e), 2012), 161; but others like it could have been found in any number of other writings representing roughly the same tendency.

4

Transgression for Anti-Fascists
On Verity Spott

During 2016 and the period of Donald Trump's first great electoral circus, the racist provocateur and ex-*Telegraph* intern Milo Yiannopoulos traveled around US university campuses giving stump speeches under the heading "The Dangerous Faggot." The talks were all structured around a kind of Coué method done in reverse. Just as the French self-help pioneer Emile Coué thought that his patients could improve their lives by repeating to themselves the refrain "every day in every way I'm getting better and better," the Yiannopoulos technique relies on the rote behaviorist insistence that the progressive opponents of his audience are getting in every way worse and worse. They are insane, immunized against facts, have nothing to say for themselves, are ugly, mentally ill, hate their lives, and are nobodies. At no other point in the whole history of far-right agitating has the role of the speaker been so explicitly therapeutic or so openly committed to making an audience feel calm with itself in its own skin. Every provocation comes packaged with an attempt to ensure that its listener "feel[s] […] confident, happy [and] reassured," as if they were babies staring up out of their cradles at the enormous benevolent faces of their fascist leaders. Every reference to the forces of progressive liberalism is calculated to remind the audience that they are nothing to worry about. For

Yiannopoulos, there can be no danger in the culture of the far-right, no risk-taking, and no transgression, before everyone, the heterosexual audience member most especially, has made sure that they are sitting absolutely comfortably. The open secret of the "dangerous faggot" is that he is the manager of a safe space.

This convergence of fascists on the therapeutic idea of self-acceptance has several interrelated motives. (1) It promotes the ongoing effort by media-savvy ethno-nationalists to stuff every available gap in the market with outright racist content. Free speech, the free-floating affect of background music, and client-centered theories of unconditional positive regard are all elements of a larger culture in which contentless feelings of gratification are the very lifeblood of its marketing operations, a fact which is exceptionally useful for customer-facing fascists whose main aim is to invest the desire to murder people and to laugh at their misfortunes with an atmosphere of reassuring familiarity. (2) The mock liberalism of psychological self-acceptance reproduces in the uplands of the human ego the same mock liberalism by means of which contemporary fascists endeavor to argue that they are merely rectifying a pattern of anti-white discrimination — the theory according to which white liberals have failed to accept their own culture, etc. In both cases this acceptance-concept is a pseudopacification of violent impulses. To tell someone that they should accept something that is fundamentally hateful is a convenient way of inflicting trauma under the auspices of its overcoming. (3) Just as classical fascism radicalizes the forms of violence required to reproduce bourgeois class relations, customer-facing fascism radicalizes the forms of psychological conformism required to accept life in a service depot. In a world in which revolutions are always made above your head and at your expense, what better coping mechanism can there be than learned hatred of the idea of transformation itself? At a low level of intensity this hatred can be named "self-acceptance" and marketed by client-centered therapists to their paying customers. At a high level it can become the working vocabulary of client-centered Nazis and serve as the basis for their campaigns against migrants and transgender people. The second ideology is only a new permutation of the first.

·

These basic reflections arise for me out of a reading of Verity Spott's poem *Click Away Close Door Say*, a work that depicts two years spent working in a private care institution in the UK while watching with mounting apprehension the insurgency of the far right across the US and much of Europe. The poem begins like this:

> I used to love to work; to come inside
> here every day, begin to move,,
>   & what that means (to assume
> a false beginning) is walking up
> the tiled path, a
> metal hand rail, grass
> to either side. The sign at the front a defunct
>   emblem. The company tag is bust.[1]

The language commences in what seems at first like natural speech conducted artlessly in iambic pentameter, "I *used* to *love*"; and only the construction "to work," a verb where we might ordinarily expect a substantive, disturbs the sensation of speech and meter in easy erotic symmetry. But even that interference feels relatively serendipitous, or like a retrieval of the idea of labor from self-subjugating cliché; and it binds it into a sequence of infinitives — "to love," "to work," "to move" — whose total effect is to summon into speech an impression of blissful self-direction. The pauses governed by punctuation arrive at regular intervals and enjoin a rhythm of gentle alternations, three beats and then two, three beats and then two, in which the rhapsody dedicated to wakeful activity is unified naturally with

---

1 Verity Spott, *Click Away Close Door Say* (London: Contraband, 2017), 9. All subsequent references to Spott's book are cited parenthetically in text..

the music of simple restfulness. At the third line, the pattern at first seems set to continue: "and what that means" is something else that the speaker may have "used to love"; their love for work and movement is also love for the meaning of work and movement in combination. But then a parenthesis opens in the line and the language enjambs before it has arrived at its accustomed metrical limit, "(to assume / a false beginning)," before the sentence continues in such a way as to sever the relationship of "and what that means" with what "I used to love." Instead "what that means" is identified with the more prosaic reality of "walking up / the tiled path, a / metal handrail, grass." The fantasy of the workplace as a closed environment of love, movement, labor and meaning has a hole punched into it and its deictic closure is compromised. The metrical organization of the language materials is terminated and the intricate patterning of verb sounds is travestied in the ugly half rhyming of "defunct" and "bust," themselves bringing to a close two terminal sentences that seem to repeat meaninglessly more or less the same thing, like any sequence of days in an ordinary working week: "The sign at the front a defunct / emblem. The company tag is bust."

This particular breakdown becomes a "defunct emblem" of what I think the poem is doing as a whole. *Click Away Close Door Say* is the largescale depiction of a breakdown in a workplace and of the various efforts of corrupt suasion and bullying used to make people shut up and fucking accept it. It is, also, a wild commentary on the fascist media talking over our heads; a more perceptive account of their baleful symmetries than can be acquired from the most admired journalistic accounts of either; an anti-case study written in furious infidelity to the idea, so central to the bumptious marketing-principles of the genre, that the lives of vulnerable people must be either larger than life or else worth nothing at all; an anti-workers' inquiry on the verge of screaming; and a confession. Where it plays out is a "specialist support service" in Hove that "looks after young adults with high functioning autism and related diagnoses / mixed diagnoses." The service belongs to a larger group of private care homes that in turn was purchased by the private equity firm Advent International in 2011 and re-sold for a £500 million profit in 2016 to the US healthcare group Acadia,[2] and much of the poem deals with the material harm that that £500 million profit represents, in terms of understaffing, trauma, workplace assaults, resentment and confusion, failures of care, bullying, malfunctioning of essential equipment, managerial horseshit, hopelessness and depression — in short, the whole gamut of experiences that contemporary service sector workers are obliged beamingly to accept.

> you got through
> until the reader was fucked
>   for a week & the lift was broken &
> the emergency radios were gone
>   & we were understaffed for over a
> year and you were leaking in the
>   low drops of paranoia, anger, and loss […] (18)

This is the situation in which client-centered fascists operate: where "Your dad, the pervert estate agent / washes his Milo" (49). The poem remains in its first parts predominantly an inquiry into details like these, which are, or constitute, as Spott puts it in the Note she appends to the poem, the "effect that the transition [in ownership] had on the individuals that lived in the service." Accordingly, the work spirals outwards from the space itself and into the process of its managerial restructuring, and then more generally still to the languages in which that restructuring was carried out and made to "seem okay" (53). After this, the focus shifts incongruously to the minor mid-twentieth-century US client- or person-centered therapist Carl Rogers, a figure who the poet "feel[s]" "that [they] hate" (69).

---

[2] Nicholas Megaw, "Britain's Priory Group Sold to US Healthcare Company for £1.5bn," *Financial Times,* January 4, 2016, https://www.ft.com/content/0fa13fe2-b2e3-11e5-b147-e5e5bba42e51.

During her pilgrimage across this landscape of management troubadours and clinical romancers, the poet is surprised by the fact that "change" and "movement" are ceaselessly invoked as if their value were held to be self-evident, or as if no change could ever be for the worse. At about the mid-point of the book, she quotes the following gloss by the group Wealth of Negations:

> CHANGE — Invoked in a general, unqualified sense to consecrate as natural and inevitable a particular shift of power in favour of some interests and against others. The naturalistic alibi gets more persuasive as one petty interest strings along together a series of coups: *it's the way the world is going; you can't turn back time so you'd better adapt.* Where particular change can be passed off by its partisans as Change in general, resistance to their next move is made to look like defence of an insufferable past.[3]

Why is it that contemporary fascists, rising like pimples from the backside of a specifically revolutionary ultra-nationalism, are now so deeply concerned to make sure that you're sitting comfortably? And since when was the value of Progress aggressively taken over by the factotums of companies like Advent International, as a technical vocabulary with which to dignify a business-model based exclusively on asset stripping? Implicit in the argument by Wealth of Negations is another recognition about the nature of revolutionary transformation. Four decades into a period of relentless bourgeois counter-insurgency against all of the institutions of working-class life, very few theories of Change have held out against the general current. Readiness for revolution implied willingness to die or to be utterly transformed. It was unthinkable except in a moment in which all his-

---

[3] Emphasis in the original. This definition was included alongside many dozens of other entries — on topics as diverse as "Cutting Edge" and "Facilities Management" — in the collective's volume on management-speak, available at Wealth of Negations, "TERMS & CONDITIONS (Complete and unabridged)," *Wealth of Negations,* April 4, 2015, http://www.wealthofnegations.org.

torical potential seemed as if it must be held in the balance. By contrast, readiness for "transition" of the kind that flows into the £500 million river of private equity alpha implies something else. It does not imply readiness to die or to be transformed, but readiness to be attacked, which is the particular state of preparedness that managers everywhere now refer to as "resilience." Change "invoked in a general, unqualified sense" refers to an alteration not in the basic order of social reality, and still less in the objective possibility for human freedom, but primarily in the individual's psychic powers of endurance. Farcical invulnerability is the alpha of this outlook and its omega too, and it is so deeply rooted in the daily practice of getting by that it has a vocabulary for every occasion.

As the theories of bourgeois therapists mutate insensibly into the motivational speeches of fascist service providers, the root cause of these changes emerges more and more blatantly into view. In economies in which, as we now know, the "overwhelming share of employment" is "shunted into sectors of the economy that are, perhaps by their very nature, technologically stagnant," a great translation gets underway in the culture that supplies them with a running commentary.[4] Vocabularies designed in historical periods in which more and more time was being reclaimed from necessary labor are restructured for a social milieu in which the possibility of technical revolutions of this kind becomes increasingly unthinkable, or where, as Verity Spott puts it, "in a generalisation based on feeling," "[t]he private sector […] doesn't mind being immobile" (14). In this situation revolution becomes a synonym for sclerosis — a merely verbal form of radicalism for a society entering into a period of generalized decline. Only a few grazes and flesh wounds in the syntax of progress remain to give the game away.

In *Click Away Close Door Say* the life that is "priced into" this "toxic pyramid / of fearful desire" (49) progresses inexorably to

---

4 Jason E. Smith, "Nowhere to Go: Automation, Then and Now," *The Brooklyn Rail*, March 2017, http://brooklynrail.org/2017/03/field-notes/Nowhere-to-Go.

the point of losing it, and the third section of the poem ends with a depiction of this breakdown, in a prose stripped of almost all of its rhythmic and grammatical assets:

> I do not want to walk through this door to stay inside that door to remain out here between them I do not want to have to move I want to see no one to be alone anyone everyone my time taken or given back I hate the cold and the heat the scabs and ridges wrists something back something gone no returning no extending no doors and every door. Sick of sick of what take me away take back my time my agency I want it gone // was born in the wrong body the wrong world its climates can not drop out of. What is the i-body, wait. (83)

This is the first of the poem's multiple endings, its most obvious blocked-up exit. It presents in shattered monologue a person at the brink of despair, exercising their last remaining autonomy in convulsive nihilism, by devaluing the life that they know will be taken from them anyway: "take back my time my agency I want it gone." It is the statement "I used to love to work" before it was knowingly concertinaed, the same thought with its mask of descriptive imperturbability thrown impatiently aside. Where does it play out? At first it might seem to be a thought screamed out in the privacy of a bedroom, in a mind pulled closed by depressive inertia. But then why are there two doors rather than one? Why do "I […] not want to walk through this door to stay inside that door to remain out here between them"? On second thought we find ourselves back at the poem's beginning: "out here" in the "airlock" (10) between the outer and inner doors of the private care unit, of which we had earlier received an "emotionless / diagram" (22). And in a sense the poem as a workers' inquiry, or as "emotionless diagram" of a work process, of its control mechanisms and "chokepoints," ends here, as too does the narrative of its development: in the anguished fit of "want" in which the desire to work or to remember what it felt like to love it is swallowed up and extinguished; while the elegy that succeeds it and makes up the poem's final part is at once a memorial to that desire and a form of literary recidivism, in which the impulses to dream-like abstraction that are repressed in the emotionless production of commodities for other people's use are at last given free rein.[5] But at this point another kind of development takes over in this poem, or wells up in it, and this development is not only a "hidden exit" from the despair that takes over a life that is shut into its place of employment with no way out, stuck or trapped in it, because it is also, and in a more general sense, the beginnings of another kind of approach to the whole question of what development means, in an economy in which the activities in which we receive our wages as workers appear impossible to revolutionize. It asks us: If it really is the case that contemporary client-centered fascism and its predilection for transgression amount only to a variation on client-centered ego psychology and its benign hatred for all forms of expressive negativity, then what would it mean to make transgression into the instrument of an actual, living transformation in human potential? The poem's answer to this question only begins at the point near to its end at which its narrative undergoes a violent breakdown. Wait.

•

In her recent book about Milo Yiannopoulos and related trends in online intellectual revanchism, Angela Nagle writes of the "cult of suffering, weakness and vulnerability that has become central to liberal identity politics." "[T]he key driving force behind" this tendency, Nagle writes, "is about creating scarcity in an environment in which virtue is the currency that can make or break the career or social success of an online user in this milieu."[6] Nagle does not say very much about the environment

---

[5] For a history of workers' inquiry as a form, see Salar Mohandesi and Asad Haider, "Workers' Inquiry: A Genealogy," *Viewpoint Magazine,* September 27, 2013, https://www.viewpointmag.com/2013/09/27/workers-inquiry-a-genealogy/.

[6] Angela Nagle, *Kill All Normies: Online Culture Wars from 4Chan and Tumblr to Trump and the Alt-Right* (Winchester: Zero Books, 2017), 76.

of this environment, about its "driving force" or about its currency — no private equity firm having yet announced that it has realized a profit of 500 million virtues — but, as the life and times of Donald Trump have proven incontrovertibly, a little bit of conceptual scarcity can go a long way, and no one should ever allow a real economy to get in the way of a fictitious one. Put differently, Nagle's presentation accepts the idea that the bold "rebellion" of the far right emerges out of the exaggerated vulnerability of those on the left and justifies that response on the grounds that "the left" has created scarcity from potential abundance. This is just a roundabout way of accusing it of being both profligate and idle. At the same time, her account tacitly denies the idea that the racist and misogynist transgression of the far right is the form taken by another therapeutic cult, this time of comfort, confidence, happiness, and reassurance,[7] the object of which is to translate an attitude of petulant egoistic defensiveness into an idiom of rebellious nonconformism, the better to conceal its deep continuity with all of the other kinds of endurance training that in existing capitalist society are passed off as business development.

The image of vulnerability in *Click Away Close Door Say* also begins with fluidity, but in a quite different mode. On p. 25 of the book the theme comes up for the first time:

> Every time you move
>
>   or are still it's there.
> You are leaking. You think to yourself you
> are leaking. The containment of lives, this
> conservative sensation of motion.

It never becomes clear exactly who this "you" is, and the revision to which the poem was subjected after its first publication in *Prelude* magazine deliberately serves to hinder this particular kind of discernment, by routinely translating heterogeneous

---

[7] I am referring to Yiannopoulos's therapeutic desire, mentioned in the first paragraph, that his listeners should feel "confident, happy [and] reassured."

third- into homogenous second-person pronouns. But news of leaks tends to be related in the poem in a voice of patient tenderness, accentuated by the smoking chaos of much of the language into which the voice intrudes. And the "conservative sensation of motion" that might be associated with bodies that don't leak and that cannot because they are "contained" also seems to characterize the language in which a leaking person or persons are identified. Unlike the persons of managers, therapists, and customer-facing demagogues, *their* rhythm, the rhythm of these bodies, is regular and non-violent: "they rage in you & teeth / to leak like skin & fire /   from s / side,,,,,,   to side" (48); or "We, both & all leak." If I were to guess I would say that the person who leaks is a resident of the service and that the "leaking" of their body is a fantasy that structures their sense of reality. The very end of the poem seems to suggest this reading most candidly, when the language allows itself a lyrical address whose acceptance of the division between poet and addressee is elsewhere refracted or prohibited: "My skin / never leaked like yours does. Your skin / leaks everyday" (95). Identification with this particular kind of fluidity then becomes the primary means by which the poem organizes its sense of loving dis-integrity, against the "Rogerian" transparency of the self who is inured to harm, in line with the aggressive imperatives of an economy whose progress has been made identical with attacks upon the vulnerable. The leak is the transference of a fantasized wound to the body of the speaker who cares for the one who bears it, and moreover it is the wound of its transference. The reader is guided through this poem against and in the wake of its narrative collapse by the tenderness that characterizes it, even as that feeling is beset by guilt and the anxiety that it might slide into betrayal: "I […] wonder / whether or not I am accumulating the pain of the people I / am paid to care for in order to strengthen my position against Rogers" (69).

It's within this system of what authors like Nagle dismiss as merely "performed" vulnerability that passages like the following begin to make sense:

> .   Scatter graphs to track in daily motions, or scatter
> the fingers in the door snapped. Scatter one finger over the
>   no
>   why not a commencement of sprinkled
> skin in the buttons over your tingling digits like leaking
>   milk shut

There is something painfully tentative in these rewritings of basic figurative preoccupations: the finger "scattered" this time rather than emitted or leaked, the skin "sprinkled" and not leaked or discharged, the commencement relocated from the "body" to the "skin." Smashed into the passage I have just quoted like glass into a sink is an image of self-harm, of fingers snapped or shut into a door, so that the constant recomposition of a single image — the fingers entering the code into a door-locking mechanism — becomes the playing out of a fantasy of self-mutilation, and at the same time a kind of penance for the inadequacy of any individual permutation of the basic image-complex from which all individual instances are derived.[8] This is not the kind of self-relation that is counselled by the psychotherapists who appear in Verity Spott's workplace as authorities, the "humanistic" promotors of "client-centred" therapy, the "mature, non-defensive people" and compassionate disavowers of anything "which was coercive or pushing in the clinical relationship."[9] But nor is its violence turned outwards towards a figure of war-

---

8   The mutilation may originally have not been self-mutilation: the first allusion to it occurs on p. 11, when Spott writes "So your hand gets / caught between the handle / and the wood, dull / pain. Your service manager wonders wistfully / if your stuck hand is an act of protest / to somehow discredit his efforts" (11). In this case what is described is a workplace accident, the kind of thing that might then have to be "populated" in the scatter graph of a risk assessment, perhaps by the same person who has already suffered the accident the "risk" of which she is expected to assess. But the constant, compulsive reproduction of variants of the image still seems to me like a more deliberate act of self-harm. Pain becomes supererogatory in relation to the demands of description.

9   The quote is from Carl R. Rogers, *On Becoming a Person: A Therapist's View of Psychotherapy* (Boston: Houghton-Mifflin, 1961), x.

ranted hatred, like George Osborne in Verity Spott's earlier work *Gideon* or David Cameron in Lucy Beynon and Lisa Jeschke's *David Cameron: Theatre of Knife Songs*.[10] I want to slam my hand in a fucking door. The wish underlies language's creative activity like concrete beneath linoleum. In Brecht's *The Measures Taken,* four party agitators sent to China to prepare the Communist revolution learn through experience that the excessive moral idealism of their young comrade will jeopardize their mission. They shoot him and throw him into a lime pit, "so that the lime will burn away all traces of you."[11] For Brecht it was the role of political art to train the mind to overcome its internalized habits of sentimentalization: to see by means of a remorseless dislocation of perspective the historical damage inflicted by the romanticism of nonviolence. Is this realization a stage in my "self actualization" as a "person," a part of my overall "effective personality change"? Can it be recuperated like this, into the digit of a code that we use to make ourselves swing open? I want to leak my hand into a fucking door.

The desire to inflict this kind of pain is not in itself uncommon. For example, attempts at self-harm can be a common behavioral trait in those diagnosed with high-functioning autism, the people for whom Verity Spott was "paid to care" (69) during the period of employment that her poem describes. Recent historical transformations in the ideology of psychiatric care or social work have led, among other things, to a gradual turn away from the most brutal procedures for stymieing this kind of self-harm, including the use of "aversive stimuli" that mimic and exceed the self-punishment they are designed to "disincentivise."[12]

---

10 Verity Spott, *Gideon* (Brighton: Barque Press, 2014).

11 Bertolt Brecht, *The Measures Taken and Other Lehrstücke* (New York: Arcade Publishing, 2001), 33. "Then we shot him and / Cast him down into the lime-pit / And when the lime had swallowed him up / We turned back to our work."

12 These "developments" in therapeutic technique are described at some length in Steve Silberman's history of the diagnostic category of autism, *Neurotribes: The Legacy of Autism and the Future of Neurodiversity* (New York: Penguin Random House, 2015), 308–15.

In Verity Spott's workplace the poet is instructed to "Ensure the erasure of punitive approaches," or, since it seems unlikely that any actual training manual would have used that phrase exactly, then she is at least instructed to avoid them; and in place of curative violence, the idea of progress as incentive is introduced, variously embellished into a jabber of pep talk along the lines of "we make things possible" (23), that we need to be "going forward" (29), to be realizing the idea of "Change in general" (38), improving through "forward motion and training" (43), practicing "self-actualization" (67), and in general committing ourselves to the "anomalous flow" of one or another kind of virtuous cycle (92).

This is the managerial language-screen through which life clinging to its need for transformation is forced to look out. The life that wakes up broken and stupid, for which "fags condense the neglected breakfast" (34) before a shift starts at "7:26am" (11), that blurts out "Fuck life" (22) and thinks of itself as "a hole to the broken / slot" (56); a self that "shout[s] back at [itself] for help" (69) and that can't sleep (81) and whose metaphors can never climax as symbols but which instead stir nauseously like acid on the stomach — this is the self who is also compelled to self-actualize in a meeting with its line manager. The juddering repetitions throughout *Click Away Close Door Say,* the evidence of text cut and pasted in a word processor and pushed around like food on a plate, the self-plagiarisms and doublings back, are the material signs of a years-long attempt to rip the poem's master metaphor out of its frame, the "central fucking door, / object of completion" (58), to slam that door shut and to kick open some other means of egress, some hidden exit. What all of those cuts and reversions mount up towards is the terms of an argument the exact internal relations of which remain undecided, but which *must* remain undecided, not simply because ambiguity is in itself fundamentally preferable to clarity, but because the conditions in which self-discovery is undertaken are the conditions of a contemporary workplace where meaning can either be snatched at or fully abjured, and because through the central fucking door and at the top of the staircase of genuine self-actualization that leads away from it, abjuration shines and gasps like a neon no-entry sign.

So much of the language of this book is defined by compulsive reworking of materials that could only be produced in conditions of fragmentation. The earlier draft of the first of the book's four parts that was published in *Prelude* is conspicuously more personal, more defiantly self-assertive, than the version that was finally included in the edition published by Contraband. Names of co-workers in the *Prelude* version are redacted in the Contraband version with a black line; the third-person pronouns used to refer to residents of the support unit are crammed into an overpopulated second-person "you"; while brilliant descriptive passages like the following are aggressively truncated:

> The regional manager overheard me on the phone joking that I am "just a support worker," which, following my failed attempts to become an academic, musician, poet, entomologist, B2B Comms worker and terminally a senior support worker, I felt was, although a joke, at least realistically fitting. She exclaimed "you're not just a support worker," to which I replied that I also write poetry and make music when my time allows me to. We haven't got on well; she isn't often there (since the Care and Quality Commission inspection in April.[13]

The parenthesis that intervenes towards the end of this passage and which is never shut up is a premonition of the more comprehensive cut to come. In a general sense these deletions are a mediated expression of the difficulty of returning again and again to a language of passionate speech that is distinguished by virtue of the fact that it is not allowed to flow, is not allowed that luxury, reserved to pensioned and / or independently wealthy

---

[13] Verity Spott, "We Make Things Possible," *Prelude Mag* 3 (2016), https://preludemag.com/issues/3/we-make-this-possible/.

poets,[14] of unbroken, natural song, but which is instead split up and interrupted by the suspended sentence of a shift pattern, or left like "Glue traces on the elbow | of the wound in our creepy head" (49).[15] This glue that thought is like, which we first encountered on the fingers inserted into every button of the door lock "like a gluey mask" (13), begins here to look like the clue it rhymes with, a creepy purloined letter "unevaporated" between my fingers like anti-bac gel, or blood by any other name: not flowing from the wound but gumming it up or joining its edges together. And the deeper into the poem you go the more these "clues" begin to hemorrhage: "When you've been subject to abuse / you might probe / it into your speech, taking each eye / to gauge whether or not what has happened is of / consequence / in the external world" (23); or 27 pages later, "When you've been a victim of / abuse you might drop hints into conversations / to see if the kindness you're getting from others sticks to you" (50). Sticks like glue? The poetry offers no immediate answer to this question; it only opens up a path into its "leaking world," descending like a helter-skelter through the fissures in a vocabulary in which the ordinary exposition of a self—which is to say of its ascent upwards, "through the echelons to constitute / the defunct 'I'"—terminates invariably in a workplace disciplinary.

But where does transgression come into all this? I wrote the first draft of this piece in 2017, at a time when my claim that the far-right aesthetic of transgression was essentially therapeutic seemed to me to be relatively speculative and controversial. In the period since, Milo Yiannopoulos has been replaced in the pantheon of the contemporary far-right by an actual author

---

14 Or as the poet Anne Boyer puts it, "There are years, days, hours, minutes, weeks, moments, and other measures of time spent in the production of 'not writing'. Not writing is working, and when not working at paid work working at unpaid work like caring for others, and when not at unpaid work like caring, caring also for a human body, and when not caring for a human body many hours, weeks, years, and other measures of time spent caring for the mind [...]": *From Garments against Women* (London: Mute, 2016), 44.

15 Also: "the removal / of life force and body from narration" (27).

of self-help books. The argument now seems thoroughly obvious and even banal. But what would an anti-fascist category of transgression look like? What does it look like in *Click Away Close Door Say*?

In order to answer that question, it may be worth taking a step back. One thing that Verity's book was meant to do was, in her own words, to begin to develop something like a "social poetics of work and mental health" (92). In its form as a scuttled workers' inquiry, her poem serves this communal aim, of elaborating a vocabulary in which we might begin to speak together about shared forms of damage, and of the shared means by which we can begin to face up to them. But the language of the poem is also just so fucking disorienting: its complex of symbols, as they grow into one another and become more and more closely inosculated — like the image of trees on the cover of Verity's earlier *Trans* Manifestos*[16] — begins to thicken and warp into something that resembles pain. And another aim slowly begins to transgress, or to betray, this primary desire to produce something coherent enough and generalizable enough to be called a "poetics" — a new aim, one that couldn't be so clearly anticipated in the first lines or pages of the poem in which it begins to well up. It insinuates itself into the shared language that the poem develops, into its key words and fundamental concepts, corrupting them and turning them to more individual purposes. The shared language of punctured ego boundaries, overcoming of the self, beautiful leaking bodies, dreams, and mutual care comes to feel at some level like a betrayal — and a new imperative betrays itself. We must disclose inadvertently the experience that no one can share with us entirely: must leak it out. In *Click Away Close Door Say* the recession in the speaking subject occurs through a self-betrayal within the work of self-overcoming, the leak within the leak. To drown in its hidden exit feels like this:

---

16 Verity Spott, *Trans* Manifestos* (Cambridge: Shit Valley, 2016).

[…] on the corner of Albumen Road in Telford, I met a man called Scüth. Or was it Halifax. I was walking alone so Scüth appeared. He was from Britain with a British accent and the first thing I knew about him was that he was suspicious … ~~Yiannopoulos~~ Scüth would sit across me from me in his clothes the only ones he wore and would read the paper but for the two holes prised out his eyes poking through them […] I explained everything to him how my school had been where it was but sat on the floor to tell him for he beneath his coat fingered a pistol perhaps that's what I suspected. He'd peer at me around corners, so I filed them down. I should have filed for a divorce but filed the corners of the house and even then noticed one day a tiny rip in his coat where he was leaking. Now why did he leak? What was he on that he leaked something out of himself while he lived there looking suspect. A pause in the brief wind […] (90–91)

It hurts for me to read this passage. It hurts because it reduces an image of tenderness to a generic trope. It blocks out the care expressed in "Your beautiful body is leaking" and flattens it into the idle clichés of a mass-market horror novel in paperback. The poem will end a few pages later with another horror sequence, when its speaker describes herself murdering an ego psychologist called Tom Kitwood by cutting through his brain stem — "The hacking / is the last taboo in me" — and then with her explaining how "When I was small […] I had something taken from me that I didn't know that I'd ever know I had" (95), and so there's a sense in which this passage is only the impersonal adumbration of a traumatic personal experience. On "Albumen Road" (albumen is the protective and nutritive layer of liquid in an egg), in the domestic environment, a seedy down-at-heel lodger whose name sounds sort of like "cut" or "scuff," and who is also the fascist Milo Yiannopoulos, leaks his concealed essence. But the writing in this passage is, or it has become, more hurtful for me than the conclusion, not only because it stages the moment when an abusive desire reveals itself in the scene of protective domesticity, but also and more catastrophically because it does so in exactly the vocabulary that the poem has enjoined us with all of its prodigious resources of metrical intelligence and at the very limits of its spectrum of anger and solicitude to hold onto or to trust. Leaking is beautiful, it is at once the sign of and the resolution to harm, we, both & all leak. It is a poetics of work and mental health that promises a language more sensitive to our estranged, damaged, fantasizing, and incontinent lives than any previous form of workers' inquiry ever has or could — and it is also just one more fucking generality that lets us down like all the others. Each of these feelings is true and each transgresses the boundaries of the other.

What is a real act of transgression? Earlier I said that the poetry's manipulation of its language materials was consistently accompanied by an image, or un- or half-conscious fantasy, of self-harm, and that that fantasy was sustained and inspissated by the need for transformation in excess of the change that any particular dislocation in language was capable of attaining. I tried to argue that that kind of abdication of self-care was beautiful, because it resumes the need for life contained in linguistic transformation on a higher plane and with a greater prospect of joy and mutual recognition. But a mark of the difficulty of this poem is that it then goes on to raise this dialectic of transformative need and self-harm to a still higher level of organization, replaying it in relation to the category that comes closest to offering us a hidden exit from fascist aggression and from the patter of psychological self-acceptance on which that bullshit now models itself. The "last taboo" in us really does here feel as if it might have been violated, rather than merely invoked in order to dignify one or another preexisting prejudice (e.g., there are only two genders). There can be no meaningful transgression in art that does not raise in us spontaneously and irresistibly beyond all of our capacities to repress it this sensation of having been violated; and at this point I really do begin to wonder, and the pain and the anxiety I feel in this passage formulates itself into a question, and the question overruns my ability to think clearly and works its way into my anxious, trivial dreams: maybe this shouldn't have been done, maybe that taboo ought to have remained intact, in the dream of care for the vulnerable whose fantasies of leaking we share. And isn't that dream enough? Why do we need to betray it? What possibility of transformation can justify the experience of groundlessness or needlessness that that betrayal can give rise to, and how can we know that it won't lead to nothing but pain, to "pain [...] without emollients of world"?[17] Is there any way in this world of not being in love with pain? Do I need to take this final step?

Any work that allows us to answer "yes" to this final question without anxious reservations must have failed to place its world under significant duress. Only in poetry where we feel acutely that in this final step we cannot say whether the ground will open up beneath the foot that is poised in midair or the foot that is planted on the ground can we know in turn that its movement is real and not fake. The vapid pretense of transgression has never in my lifetime represented a greater threat than it does now: principles that barely exist in the world and for whose reality we need to fight get raised up on stilts of violence as the main dogmas of our entire culture, so that the act of tearing them down comes to look like daring freedom from illusion. Fuck all of the people who think that this is a way to struggle against the reality that makes us begin our attempt to talk about our lives in the language of what we used to love. I love this poem, I think it is unforgettable; no one will ever be comfortable in it; and it is because and not in spite of this fact that the love that leaks from its entire body betrays itself without any guarantees that it will pour out towards its end.

---

17 The full quotation from the description on the publisher's page — written by the poet Will Rowe — is as follows: "The writer is a carer in an institution where the normativity function of world, its disposition of space, occurs as a containment of death. Human empathy in this environment is an irruption of uncontainable disorder. To look at this place produces deep disorder inside: how can one live there? How long is it possible to live at an extreme edge, this kind of edge? The answer relates to truth, sheer insistence on truth, without any resolution by hope. That means pain, without emollients of world." *Click Away Close Door Say* by Verity Spott, Contraband: Modernist Poetry Press, https://www.contrabandbooks.co.uk/product/click-away-close-door-say-by-verity-spott/.

5

World History's Teenage Diaries: On Lisa Jeschke

Ever since Margaret Thatcher said her thing about there being "no alternatives," the political situation has been analyzed in terms of an absence of good options. We know all about this absence, ritualized in another text about that in centered alignment, lasting four minutes, written by a different person each time similarly disposed of. It is the gap in the market that never stops selling, if not quite what it was then so much the better.[1]

If I want to make an argument about this absence then I need to add to it some extra terms. (1) It is easy to feel that there are no good options, but it is difficult to feel passionate for bad ones. (2) The painstaking metamorphosis of bad options that fall below the threshold of good politics goes on slowly and only through the cold fronts of isolation and self-loathing. (3) It is also the only way in which our total situation can evolve to the point at which good options are once again available to be fought for. (4) When Marx wrote that "Right can never be higher than the economic structure of society and its cultural

---

[1] I am thinking, in case it isn't clear, of any piece of left-wing web "content" that tells you before you look at it that it's a "four-minute read."

development which this determines," he was historically and not only incidentally wrong.[2]

This essay, focusing on some recent poetry by Lisa Jeschke, will be about the effort to identify with bad options, which is to say that it will be about the experience, not of resignation to bad options, but of feeling oneself to be attacked and overwhelmed by a kind of ludicrous, embarrassing passion for them, against all of the strictures and dictates of healthy common sense. In this connection it will also develop some thoughts about the meaning of the phrase "to each according to their needs, from each according to their ability" in relation to work carried out on language, and it will set out a brief epitaph for those orthodox observers of determination who think that this connection is trivializing and illegitimate, on the grounds that it says nothing about the transformation of the economic structure. It is this part of the text that will seem most clearly to address current affairs, since the clearest evidence of the failure of that narrow orthodoxy is right now instated in the narrow racism of ex-communist opponents of the EU, whose apparently epistemological indifference to culture reveals itself over time as nothing more than the expression of a repressed resentment for those who make it, stripping off the last vestiges of its Marxism and nakedly committing itself to "British culture and values," which is a dignified way of saying to British racism and British pedophilia scandals.

Aside from this immediate purpose, the essay also has another, broader aim. I want to try to say in a larger sense some-

---

[2] Karl Marx, *Critique of the Gotha Program*, in *Collected Works of Marx and Engels* (London: Lawrence & Wishart, 2010), 24:87: "But these defects [of distributional justice] are inevitable in the first phase of communist society as it is when it has just emerged after prolonged birthpangs from capitalist society. Right can never be higher than the economic structure of society and its cultural development which this determines." Marx was right to ridicule Lassalle's belief in the independent power of the state in relation to working-class self-activity, but he was wrong to interpret this activity in strictly "economic" terms. It is the collapsing of the first term into the second that leads to the idea that political institutions can disappear "of themselves" (24:92).

thing about how it feels right now in this part of 2018 to want change: to drive that desire deeply into our habits of perception and instinct. The difficulty of doing this seems to me to be related to the kind of relationship to language that the technical means of communication now imposes. As the drive to bring about, rather than to comment or to report on, change in language is withdrawn, the category itself seems to recede and to lose its historical dimensions. I cannot do conceptual thinking when I am confronted or satiated with language on a screen like this — although fatally I can still feel interested in it — and this blurring of thought and the interest into which it decays is itself a part of the tonality of language, as it tries to communicate the most radical potential of concepts and aspirations that have been contorted in their social inheritance. I mean also that I love people who wreck and torture language, because in the encounter with their own refracted needs the whole history of what we can no longer candidly mean seems to burst back into the concepts that I otherwise can waste days staring at in a stupor of imperceptiveness. I realize that this should be put more clearly.

•

To think clearly it is necessary to have examples. As I write this it is almost two years since the EU referendum that has determined the recent direction of British politics. The "No" vote that secured a 52 percent majority among those who turned out has introduced a very large transformation in immediate political realities, and a large change too in institutional structures. Some of the immediate aftermath of these changes makes up the subject of Lisa Jeschke's poem "Eurotrash," which begins like this:

> On 25 June 2016, walking through a London valley of great nature,
> Thoughts wandering along with feet: left right and centre
> I chanced upon the sight of a monstrous maiden bumhole singing

> Who she was clearly drunk, definitely from the EU, slurring
> I was enchanted, and I stopped, and listened to those sub-
>   waged i-tunes
>
> Streaming from her mouth light
> *Right into the low-cost maintenance mouldy tubular interiors*
>   *of my ear*[3]

What kind of change in the historical sense of transformation can language like this communicate? In an immediate confrontation with this poem the question seems unreal. The lines are, or they appear like, a mockery protruding from a mockery. The opening lines do not only mock the thoughts of the solitary speaker but also the comic practice of mismatched registers as such. "On 25 June 2016, walking through a London valley of great nature" is not a comic displacement of the experience of the urban pedestrian into the mode of the Romantic solitary, but the deliberate sabotage of that very mode of satirical displacement. Its opening line is a farcically awkward version of what in a more recognisable mode of light pastiche might have gone

> On 25 June 2016, as golden noon,
> visiting the spring, descended across the city's
> streets and rented houses,
> I learned [...]

---

[3] Lisa Jeschke, "Eurotrash," in *Look at Hazards, Look at Losses,* eds. Group for Conceptual Politics, Anthony Iles, and Marina Vishmidt (London: Mute Publishing, 2017), 122. Emphasis in original. Further references cited parenthetically in the main text. Note that it's impossible to give the title correctly here because it should really be in size 24-point font. This also applies to various other poems in the collection. The poems by Lisa Jeschke in *Look at Hazards, Look at Losses* were later republished in an expanded edition as *The Anthology of Poems by Drunk Women* (Cambridge: Materials, 2018).

or whatever; and the possibility of that improvement, which in fact would be a neutralization, is a part of what the lines mean, so that the subjective pressure involved in their statement is not annulled or dissipated but is instead sublimed or debased into the mere effort of leaving them as they are. The sense of the lines is dominated by the possibility of not saying them, or by the frenzy of desire for dis-utterance held consciously in abeyance, despite the clamor of the mind for a second referendum on their legitimacy.

Lisa Jeschke's texts in *The Anthology of Poems by Drunk Women* are often variations on this kind of ritual of self-humiliation. They assert themselves as language whose characteristic crudities and leaps of theatrical self-exposure mean that the hardest thing for their author to do is to leave them exactly as they are. Many of the poems concern surveillance by the state, the superego, medical professionals, or by some combination of all three (cf. "Prime / Dentist" (126), of which more later), and all of these forms of oversight blur into one another and form a continuum. Images of shame or humiliation accumulate implacably: the poems say things like "The Alpine rivulets blushed," or they exclaim in agonies of impotent mortification that "Frauke Petry / I do not want you to read / Uh, my teenage diaries" (124). Throughout their development of these basic themes the poems carry out numerous crude experiments in typographical emphasis, enjamb in the wrong places, fatten with filler, excrete emoticons, make preposterous, juvenile declarations of unguarded woundedness, rhyme excruciatingly, and suffer under their own embarrassing illocutionary force. Furthermore, they do all of this while swimming in a second language whose inherent risks of self-exposure are explored by the poet to their very depths of alarm and aphasic cataplexy. In the perverse radicalism of their refusal to change, and more particularly in the radicalism of their adherence to what is ugly, sclerotic, ridiculous, or embarrassing, the inner logic of the poetry might at first seem hard to fathom. It may not seem to provide any means of thinking clearly about, or even of feeling decisive in relation to, our present political moment. But then by the same reason it is hard from the outside to fathom the radicalism of the desire to maintain unchanged an ugly, sclerotic, ridiculous, and embarrassing institution such as the EU.

·

For anyone not yet entranced by the ugly, sclerotic, and ridiculous institution Nigel Farage, the current state of European politics does not inspire any sense of revolutionary optimism. Instead, it compels a sense of organizational confusion, a loss of aim and uncertainty, or of painful isolation — a feeling of moving uncomfortably through a reality that has itself snapped into a new form, in which the old kinds of action no longer make sense. Poetry written in these circumstances is unhappy poetry. It carries titles such as *Our Death,* or *The Anthology of Poems by Drunk Women*.[4] And the feeling has objective grounds and is not just an effusion of defeatist irrationalism attributable to over-sensitive poets. In fact, the lesson of both of the books whose titles I just mentioned is that the feeling can be cognitively and expressively worked on — that it can be stretched out into abstract diagnoses or compacted into simple questions. It is itself a space of possibility even if it is inseparable from despair, and its terrain is at the moment vastly more expansive than the terrain, almost entirely theoretical and largely nostalgic, in which we feel capable of stating with confidence how unnecessary deprivation can be brought to an end.

I feel another problem adjacent to this one. The problem is about who I am to say any of this. If Marx and Engels's great breakthrough in the manuscripts that would be published a century later as *The German Ideology* was to discover that German philosophy had to be abandoned in favor of direct analysis of

---

4   *Our Death* is the title of a recent sequence by Sean Bonney, some of which is published in his recent book, *Ghosts* (London: Materials, 2017). "We were talking about prophecy, about defeat and war, about how nobody knows what those words really mean, and what they will come to mean."

social being,[5] our own period compels a comparable transformation: not this time the translation of the language of political economy into the definition of "the subject," but of the drunk and physically damaged life into the world in which political economy is the dominant means of coordinating production and of reproducing class power. I feel this compulsion as a kind of faint urge, to burst into the reality whose description in both conservative and radical vocabularies is so drably familiar, and is most drably familiar of all where it professes to identify as a part of that reality a corresponding form or structure of subjectivity. The merely individualist or petty-minded question "where am I in all of this" is in this sense the central problem for a living political vocabulary, and the issue of how to pose it is the central technical task for any poetry that wishes to make use of the enormous resources of our own living experience of loss or marginality or speechlessness or poverty or dissolution or physical pain. To learn to sweep through all of those experiences and to grasp their proximity to (or their distance from) the implacable event of capitalist institutional reality is right now the only way in which poetry as a medium can offer any kind of concerted resistance to the rise of a sneering and pacifying right-wing vocabulary whose entry into our immediate political environment is not only the result of a failure by the left to take advantage of a global economic crisis, but also of a collapse in our ability to contest in language the travestying of the impulses that underlie our political positions. Put differently: I think that fascism will continue to flourish for so long as those

---

5   See the introductory essay in Marcel van der Linden and Gerald Hubmann, *Marx's* Capital: *An Unfinishable Project?* (Leiden: Brill, 2018): "previous editions [of *The German Ideology*] suggested the existence of a finished 'work,' in which the philosophy of historical materialism is supposed to have been elaborated. In contrast, textual reconstruction of the unfinished manuscripts in the MEGA² reveals that the true concern of Marx and Engels was a critique of post-Hegelian philosophy. This did not — as previous editions would have it — culminate in the elaboration of the philosophy of historical materialism, but rather in the revocation of philosophy and the abandonment of philosophical discourse in favour of politics and economy" (21).

of us who oppose the preservation of class society are unable to insist that the theoretical positions with which we are identified are *our* positions and not the dreams and fantasies of manikins and caricatures. We have to make the fact of that identification as visceral and as breathtakingly complex as it is capable of being made.

Why should this be a problem that we are particularly compelled to confront now? Is it simply because the increasingly oblique relationship of our political concepts to mass practice demands that we confront our own personal relationships to them? Or is it because the current sequence of political events, the EU negotiations, rise of anti-migrant movements, the aftereffects of economic crisis, feels like a rerun of the politics of the 1970s, only with the workers' movement brutally edited out? Provisional answers to those historical uncertainties might be derived by way of a more personal sequence of questions: Can I defend communism by publicly expressing my inclination to feel sick of it? Can I re-vindicate a concept that has been emptied of social reality by living as graphically as possible the pain we feel when we see it travestied? For the very upright left-wing advocates of British resistance to the single market in the 1970s, questions like these would have sounded disgracefully subjectivist if not simply incomprehensible, just as, in another sense, the writings of feminists and gay rights activists sounded to them like a ridiculous distraction from the real business of, for example, challenging the power of the right wing in Britain's military apparatus.[6] The writers of that tendency who are still

---

6   Many of the arguments now conducted in British culture about the nature of the European Union were had in not dissimilar terms in the mid-1970s. And yet the almost perfect reversal of the poles of the exchange, so that in 1975 the desire to exit the Common Market was the uniform position of the majority of the left, while in 2016 it was the uniform position of the majority of the right, seems to encapsulate the historical transformations of the past forty years, as well as to add credence to the view, expressed with great regularity by contemporary fascists with ties and webcams, that the positions of the left have drifted in the direction of the status quo. If the EU continues to be a "eurostomach" that, as E.P. Thompson wrote in 1975, will, "Once replete […] want to euronate" on the working class; and

alive today collude with Nigel Farage and Boris Johnson in reviving a kind of diluted national socialism in which the vision of popular control of the commanding heights is streamlined into a single proposal to nationalize the declining British sphincter, for commingled reasons of sentiment and state. This is what they mean by their slogan about "taking back control."[7] They are people like the ex-communist Bob Rowthorn,[8] who collaborates with the red-brown thinktank Civitas[9] in publishing

---

if in 1971 "as large a *rassemblement* of popular forces as one could wish for," including "most of the trade unions, most of the working class, most of the Labour Party, the CPGB, the anarchists, the underground, the pacifists, the marxist groupuscules, and most of the 'unorganized' left-wing intelligentsia" "came together to oppose the Common Market," as Thompson's adversary Tom Nairn announced — then how to explain the current left-wing support for an institution that over the last thirty years has acquired, in addition to its original eurostomach, a whole troika of institutional rumens, reticulums, and funds, and that has spent the entire duration of the financial crisis chewing with its mouth open? See E.P. Thompson, "Going into Europe," in *Writing by Candlelight* (London: Merlin, 1980), 86, and Tom Nairn, *The Left Against Europe?* (Harmondsworth: Penguin, 1973), 122.

7   That is to say that the phrase is not just a dog-whistle; though of course it is that too, and its psychological or therapeutic connotation is in any case inseparable from its sotto voce racist camaraderie ("take back control *of our borders*").

8   In the 1980s Rowthorn was a prominent Gramscian proponent of import-controls as part of a strategy of socialist economic transformation. His article from the January 1981 edition of *Marxism Today* on "The Politics of the Alternative Economic Strategy [AES]" continues to be cited from time to time as the best overview of the economic strategy developed by the broad far left; http://banmarchive.org.uk/collections/mt/pdf/81_01_04.pdf. His incredulous assertion that groupuscules still further to the left considered the AES to be "authoritarian, reformist, impractical and chauvinistic" now seems remarkably prescient (5).

9   Rowthorn's dreary and alarmist report *The Costs and Benefits of Large-Scale Immigration* (London: Civitas, 2015) can be found without difficulty by anyone who has a good reason to do so. Its "findings" were widely cited in the right-wing British newspapers, which of course is the whole reason for the existence of the report in the first place, as well as for the opaquely funded think tank that commissioned it. Rowthorn's derisive concession that immigration "may [!] also bring benefits such as a more varied cuisine" seems to stiffen into a more academic phraseology the outright taunts of David Coleman, with whom he has cowritten an academic arti-

alarmist "economic" prognostications in which Britain becomes so full of migrants that it collapses into the sea; or his ex-social democrat colleague David Goodhart, who argues that the real division in British society is not a division in class but between two "large value blocks" of which the larger is primarily defined by hostility to "change."[10]

I am sick of these people and of their communism which is also mine, a sinew twisted into it and impossible to rip out. I want to hate more and more graphically the devastation of the concepts that now collapse into resentful anxiety about borders and the impoverished people who die on the wrong sides of them, and I want the sickness to be historical, a lesson learned in the nerves from the intricate history in which the desire for communism pursued through struggle led to so many accomplishments beyond our power of anticipation. I want the sickness to flare up in the communism that sickens me by virtue of its exclusion of exactly that sensation, along with so much else of what happened in the period that separates the present from its decades-old doppelganger. What is there now besides bad options? What drift and snap of popular energy, what acts of theft, what effrontery, what chiaroscuro, what warping of

---

cle, and who in 2003 asserted that the benefits of immigration were "rather difficult to specify beyond a wider range of ethnic restaurants for the middle classes and new kinds of pop music for youth." Coleman is, among other things, a member of the eugenicist Galton society and was recently involved in a fight around a eugenics conference at University College London. His variety of respectable British racism opposes the EU and exists in an ever-closer union with outright neo-Nazism. For more on some of this background, see Beth Davies-Kumadiro, "Eugenics Is Not a Fringe Issue — It Influences UK Immigration Policy," *Novara Media,* January 13, 2018, https://novaramedia.com/2018/01/13/eugenics-is-not-a-fringe-issue-it-influences-uk-immigration-policy/. For the Coleman quote, see David Pallister, "The Numbers Game," *The Guardian,* March 21, 2007, https://www.theguardian.com/commentisfree/2007/mar/21/themarsbarhasa.

10 Rowthorn is a particularly interesting case because there exists a very lively depiction of him in the 1960s memoirs of Sheila Rowbotham, a brilliant socialist-feminist scholar who in no way has shared his trajectory. See Rowbotham's *Promise of a Dream: Remembering the Sixties* (London: Verso, 2002).

cupidity or sexual withdrawal, what cacophony, what chants, what organizational breakthroughs, what damage inflicted on the latest corporate-technical whatever, what nihilism and what utopianism, what fights in the street, what depression and what euphoria, what self-mythologization, what dreams, what compromise between communication and screaming, what level of intensity, what pattern of self-harm, what conflict between individualism and collectivity, what psychological desublimation, what repression, what taste for abstraction or concretion, what arc of decline, what unspoken impulses twisted into sarcasm and what collisions between different cultures, genders, ethnicities, styles of being together or of desire, in what shape of solidarity or enmity or both, and what love and what coldness, and what popular history, what futurism, what bile, what parties, what clothes, what anticipation or memory projected into nature, what rain and what heat, what fantasies of murder or revenge, what systems for explaining these away, what deaths and what recoveries, what developments and what regressions, what horizons and what immediacies, and what willingness to be hurt, and what cries of pain, in what tenor, at what volume, in what form, in the face of what missed opportunities or culminations, and what art and what denial of it, and what directness, and streets and signs and commerce and collectivism, and what equilibrium of pragmatism and despair, what attunement to global reality, what intoxicated immediacy, and what contortions in the attempt to realize in each of these things and in every moment of their dialectic their highest possibility?

•

The first poem in Lisa Jeschke's *Anthology* is "Operation Vanitas Eikonal Heimat Horror Poem":

> Winter's Bad Aibling's surgery oh travel
> From heart felt to heart synth. We pieces of
> Shit soon to collide from boredom at work
> The entire bodies shivered! At this arse

Of a world in this bath fixing bad bodies the
Showers were cold. The golf balls of
Industrious mountains dimensions and reach,
Ears of span through tin can, listen!

Gladly you strip ourselves. To each
The condition makes your head a skeletal
Head in your hand hehe. You are in it is dark
in the afternoon. When we die, is it organ

by organ or all at once? Will one cheek
Go first and you, Pinkie, second hoho?
The side is endlessly infra, plus x giants
Of despair, the arterial road leads out ah

FRG planners of towns, the centre
Rehabilitates neon-bright light into the night.
This is a palace of sickening health, it calls
Itself beautiful, it accumulates what? It

Globally draws, that's its thing, its twist, its
Strength. Distinctly on different planets
Huhu you waved to me and then you were
Gone. Disappeared. Hole search teams

Couldn't extension. Had a king eaten a
Human? Was it Horst S.? Now, are you
Eating him from within? Can he sleep at
Night? Lost my way. Found it! Lost it. Hum

"Better to cut myself | myself than wait for
Him to do it." No! Couldn't bear it: cut off
My tongue. The Alpine rivulets blushed, run
Soaked in blood. The blood pools looked up

In horror. And this was how we lived. And
We got out of the bath, and we returned to

> Munich was now the centre of Europe. And
> This was the turn of the year. And there was
>
> A terror warning prediction for the central
> Station. And within minutes, Pegida-Lutz
> Smug-faced how he now wanted to see the
> Welcome-clappers there. But of course
>
> We will be there, Lutz Lutz Lutz Lutz Lutz. (118–19)

The poem's title refers to "Operation Eikonal," "the first successful attempt at mass surveillance of European telecoms," which took place in Bad Aibling, Munich;[11] to the genre of renaissance still life painting that depicts the transience of human wishes; and to Nazism and slasher flicks.[12] It does so in the crudest way possible, by means of a list. The quatrains are all roughly decasyllabic and unmetrical. From time to time the text is interrupted by transcriptions of artificial laughter like you might find in a web forum or a mobile phone message ("hehe," "hoho"), or by noises that look like transcriptions of artificial laughter but which aren't ("huhu") and that on second thoughts may instead be humans with their little men cut off. Complex literary allusion and sophisticated acts of morphological displacement run up against the most simpleminded kinds of assonance and

---

11 The quote is from the Austrian member of parliament Peter Pilz and is quoted on the *Wikipedia* page for Operation Eikonal: https://en.wikipedia.org/wiki/Operation_Eikonal.

12 *The Texas Chainsaw Massacre* seems to be a particular favorite. It is an appropriate companion-object for Lisa's poetry, because so much of the horror in her writing is associated with the faces of politicians, which in our dream lives become freely detachable just as they are infinitely changeable in social reality. I recall a joke by the comedian Frankie Boyle that the Labour politician Andy Burnham had "carved Fireman Sam's face off and laid it carelessly across his own skull." This observation seems to me to be widely applicable. Frankie Boyle, "How Will Labour Top Losing the Election? By Losing Its Own Leadership Contest," *The Guardian*, August 27, 2015, https://www.theguardian.com/commentisfree/2015/aug/27/how-will-labour-top-losing-the-election-by-losing-its-own-leadership-contest.

syntactical fuck up. "Operation Vanitas Eikonal Heimat Horror Poem" (henceforth OVEHHP) is not the kind of poem that encourages its reader to take the time to find out (for example) that "x giants of despair" might be an allusion to John Bunyan's *The Pilgrim's Progress,* in which Christian and Hope are imprisoned by Giant Despair in Doubting Castle and tortured into killing themselves, even if you can find that out by a bit of Googling; and by parity of reason the poem does not encourage us to join that allusion to the two following poems with the titles "Should one commit suicide with a view to NOTHING but ARBEIT ahead?" or to the phone call to the Samaritans that is described in one of another pair of poems, each with the title "The Future." It does not try to uplift its reader into "find[ing] new ways of making language meaningful and memorable," as the boring and conservative poet Rebecca Watts stipulates that poetry should,[13] and nor does it exhaust itself in the attempt to make it "blurry, distressing, and forgettable," like Watt's brilliant radical antithesis Anne Boyer.[14] Insinuated throughout OVEHHP is a third term for this old dialectic, which recognizes that at least one of the addressees of the poetry is not a reader at all, and that it belongs to no determinable class or gender position,

---

[13] This was the credo with which Watts signed off her indignantly hedge-trimming review of the poetry of Rupi Kaur, Hollie McNish, and Kate Tempest in the *PN Review*. Highlights include the passage in which Watts demands of McNish a better explanation of her way of eating peanuts ("[i]t's not clear what's stopping McNish from putting her nuts in a bowl") and the outraged anathemas that she pronounces upon the use of brackets in book section titles ("the use of parentheses to shield the terms from scrutiny is plain insulting"). The text is a useful window onto the burning issues that animate mainstream British poetry. Rebecca Watts, "The Cult of the Noble Amateur," *PN Review* 44, no. 3 (2018), https://www.pnreview.co.uk/cgi-bin/scribe?item_id=10090. For an excellent response to Watts's text, see Momtaza Mehri, "Letters from a Young (Female) Poet," *The Millions,* January 31, 2018, https://themillions.com/2018/01/letters-from-a-young-female-poet.html.

[14] Anne Boyer, "Clickbait Thanatos: On the Poetics of Post-Privacy," in *A Handbook of Disappointed Fate* (New York: Ugly Duckling Presse, 2018), 113–18.

because it is nothing but the internationally coordinated data collection agencies of the repressive bourgeois state.

The poem is also full of dubious expressions of love, variously addressed to the state border ("oh travel"), to one's own dying, blushing cheeks, to the Federal Republic of Germany, to the Hitlerite hairdresser Lutz Bachmann, and to the vowel sound ʊ. Its mode of progression is tacitly exuberant, spiraling uncontrollably downwards from the title on, and the title already symbolizes this intoxicated will to free associative self-abandonment, "Operation Vanitas Eikonal Heimat Horror Poem" mixing up its Greek and Latin, its Hollywood and its Renaissance, its poem and its listening exercise. The overall effect is derived from the sensation not only that the work is defined by a very free kind of intellectual movement, but that it is consciously an attempt to face into and obstinately to overcome the feelings of inhibition that particular methods of movement tend to induce. Free association, internal rhyme, adventitious homophony, visual puns, etc., are all treated as ways of driving forwards a thought process that can nevertheless be blocked up by internalized standards of propriety, which is to say that the poem sees that an ersatz form of intellectual development, deeply subservient to the process of class-socialization, can in fact be defined by a systematic process of progressive self-denial, in which all of the possibilities for cognitive-expressive advance are ruthlessly sacrificed or boarded up, under the auspices of self-cultivation. Smiley face. The desire to get fucking wasted is then defined in something like these terms: obsessional over-control of language is a recipe not for a more radical and technically advanced poetry but for uptight class banality or delusional paranoia. Close reading is surveillance culture. And the more that I dwell on what lies behind the surface of this language, the more closely the language watches me do it. I am "hole search teams," noticing, for example, that in the line "Soaked in blood. The blood pools looked up" there is a recurrence of the language of internet searches (search teams "looked up" search terms) and a proliferation of "oo" vowels that glare back out at me from the lines like a swarm of staring eyes. "In my back and on my back / An eight-eyed thing is watching me / At once and in rotation" (121).

In order to understand what is happening here, it is necessary to understand something about embarrassment. In the evolution of the contemporary poet, embarrassment has a particular developmental role. For the majority of trained poets, embarrassment at the historical claims that have been made for verse is primeval. Shelley's unselfconscious skylark is the poet's primary evolutionary form, and it is only after many hundreds of years spent mutating in a graduate program that this primitive organism acquires its developed characteristics as a kind of polychromatic bipedal clown, whose conceptual buffoonery and outsized shoes are so fetching. The laughable, arch, ridiculous, and always self-conscious poems that emerge from the contemporary MFA system represent so many complex expressions of this history, and they search out ever new ways of conveying the knowledge that they themselves must be laughable and ridiculous simply by virtue of their position in a lineage of historical types. At its worst, this knowledge degrades poetry to a series of banal pranks on expressive aspiration, the flipside of which is an enthusiastic endorsement of the capitalist organization of cultural experience. At its best, it turns poetry into a kind of dreamwork, the sensitive metamorphoses of which still suggest at some level a kind of repressive self-constraint.

But Lisa Jeschke's embarrassment is *not like this*. Embarrassment is the aim of the poetry and not the atmosphere in which it breathes. The laughter that happens in it is not the knowing laughter of the audience brought up to want its own propensity for self-effacement to be knowingly and reassuringly confirmed; it is a sarcastic, bodily noise like gargling, intended to make posh cunts like them feel uncomfortable. Its quotient of redundant distortion echoes in solidarity the meaningless sounds that bodies make under the stress of a life over which their subjects have too little control to do anything besides try to hold on, and which in the end is more accurately expressed anyway when it is communicated as a cry than when it is flattened into a diagram, a parallelogram of forces, or even a narrative. Her poetry develops for the twenty-first century the historical intuition of Rimbaud, who so desperately wanted in his *A Season in Hell* to be "The drunken gnat in the urinal of an inn, smitten with borage, dissolved by a shaft of light," and it does this by grasping at whatever breakdown or vicissitude of sensation is forced beneath the threshold of history or even of experience itself, and which even the faintest glimmer of the day or disturbance of the hour is sufficient completely to irradiate.[15] Her drunkenness is the state in which we pass out in our concepts, in which we wake up into the pain that they blot out, the days that they make colorless and impossible to speak of, the sickness and banalized intrusions of whatever makes up a life on the edge of speechlessness, bits of phonetic detritus of the kind that you can rip out from the Christian name of some fascist who we would willingly drink to forget, only to wake up again into new false starts and new meaningless ecstasies and find ourselves still talking, helplessly, in a language that suffocatingly denies them. It is the state in which we can continue to need to be able to say "I am a / woman / and I / need to / eat" (120) and call that a poem in spite of everything that tells you that it is an idiotic and embarrassing thing to do, because the world is full of people whose own embarrassment-concept is so much more cleverly refined; and it is the attempt to find some way to face up to a culture that is increasingly governed by populist male politicians whose en-

---

15 In Wyatt Mason's translation, the full quote is: "I loved desert, scorched orchards, sun-bleached shops, warm drinks. I dragged myself through stinking streets and, eyes closed, offered myself to the sun, god of fire.

'General, if upon your ruined ramparts a single cannon yet remains, bombard us with clods of earth. Strike shop mirrors! Sitting rooms! Feed our cities dust. Coat gargoyles in rust. Fill boudoirs with fiery, ruby ash …'

Oh! The drunken gnat in the urinal of an inn, smitten with borage, dissolved by a shaft of light! [Oh! le moucheron enivré à la pissotière de l'auberge, amoureux de la bourrache, et que dissout un rayon!]." See Arthur Rimbaud, *Rimbaud Complete*, trans. Wyatt Mason (New York: Modern Library, 2003), 211. Compare also the conclusion to "The Drunken Boat": "If I still long for Europe's waters, it's only for / One cold black puddle where a child crouches / Sadly at its brink and releases a boat, / Fragile as a May butterfly, into the fragrant dusk" (89).

dorsement of extrajudicial incarceration and mass drowning is winningly justified on the grounds that they are ordinary people who like to have a drink or two.

It is in this sense, also, a highly pressurized attempt to confront the relationship of anti-migrant anality to a regulated kind of orality. When Boris Johnson and Nigel Farage promise the workers control over their own sphincters while standing around in a pub — "*I want to drink with Boris, I want to drink with Nigel*" (122) — they take aggressive desires right out of our mouths. The psychopathological element of this speech-drama is made luridly explicit in the *Anthology* in the treatment of Horst Seehofer, leader of the Christian Social Union and my "prime / Dentist" (126),[16] since a dentist, as Jeschke knows and as Donald Winnicott formulated most clearly, is "a dangerous man […] who might take out teeth to punish you for biting," and who can furthermore insist that women who "need / to eat" do so in the most restrained and ladylike manner possible.[17] This in any case was the implication of Nigel Farage's comments on the groping scandal in Cologne on the occasion of the New Year's celebrations of 2016, in which he offered to protect the civil rights of any woman who would accept him as her moderately intoxicated spokesperson; and as I write this the point is being recycled in the mainstream news by the career Islamophobe Tommy Robinson, whose female cameraperson was yesterday knocked over by anti-fascists as they tried to prevent her from filming attendees at an anti-fascist conference. "Rather groped in Cologne / Than marry a man / That's my New Year's / Resolution" (125), Jeschke replies. And in *The Anthology of Poems by*

---

16 In an earlier poem, Seehofer eats the poem's speaker and is then eaten by this speaker from the inside. By this point, it is too late for a dental checkup.

17 D.W. Winnicott, *Holding and Interpretation: Fragment of an Analysis*, ed. M. Masud R. Khan (London: Hogarth Press, 1986), 64. "But the main thing is that our relationship was stopped by a dentist who is imaginatively a dangerous man, who might take out teeth to punish you for biting, for your cannibalistic impulses and ideas — a form of castration." Note the thoroughly ambiguous "a form."

Drunk Women we see the type of this new man rise up, a Leviathan for our time, with a smartphone for his sword and a CCTV camera for his crosier, rifling through our teenage diaries and promising to smash our teeth out, bellowing *Non est potestas Super Terram quae Comparetur* as if it were a smash hit by Sinead O'Connor, and taking up into itself our own cannibalistic urges so as to concentrate them with monomaniacal exclusivity on the poor old fleshless Statue of Liberty.

What are the historical stakes of this poetry, in which orality is not only related to its expression as song, but also to the sublimation of biting? Is it just a particularly exaggerated form of acting out — a tantrum in language, a transgression ultimately inseparable from the parental authority that it constructs? And if it is, then how do we explain its continued, passionate preoccupation with the interiors of words, with their significant blood and guts, and with the botched or painstaking surgery that the living mind can carry out on them?

I think that two distinct impulses run together in this work. On the one hand, the poetry is obsessively concerned with doing things that it shouldn't. We are familiar with that kind of transgressiveness. Our lives are organized by the petty injunctions that define it. Don't suck your thumb, don't answer back, don't start conversations with strangers on trains, don't write poems that conclude with the world "smelt" or use exclamation marks for emphasis! The poetry that defeats these prohibitions says what it needs to: it searches through the blizzard of its own sense of shame and habitual reserve for new prohibitions that it can defy. Also, it tries to *make use* of shame and embarrassment, as routes out of the state of rule-abiding civility in which all of us slope about most of the time. But where does this commitment take us? *The Anthology of Poems by Drunk Women* trials different answers to this question. At the end of the second of Jeschke's two poems with the title "Should one commit suicide with a view to NOTHING but ARBEIT ahead," she writes of Donald Trump that "we knew now what to do" (127); and what we knew "now" that we had to become, in this simulated rhetoric of bellicose decisiveness, what we needed to say that we should be, is — "More than him." More than him means more alive and more receptive and more conscious and more unconscious too: and more capable of knowing ourselves by the constant testing of the boundaries that define who we are and what we are capable of wanting. We become more than him by growing to encompass the "Total universe" (129): by being more alert and more encompassing than yesterday's and today's political manikins could ever be. And then what. The poem asks this as if innocently. "And we? Laugh, prepare. And then? And further?"[18] Jeschke doesn't answer her own question openly, but in the contrariousness of her own literary instincts an answer is nevertheless awkwardly latent. To say what we need in defiance of internalized prohibitions is one way of extending our literary vocabulary, but the movement in thought that it represents does not necessarily carry us towards any particular type of relationship to whatever it is that we say. In other words, it is possible to say what we need without saying anything about that need itself, and so the expansionary tendency in the subjectivity that throws off all prohibitions at the cost of shame or ridiculousness does not by this means necessarily say all that it can.

What does it mean to want to do all that I can with my needs, to want more from the kinds of deprivation that they express? Can I develop an oral fixation on need itself? Does it make a difference if I ask this question at 11 a.m. or 5:28 p.m.? I can stare for hours at nothing and feel frantic, and my language and the life that it has shaped look out blankly at one another: Better to be groped in Cologne than to marry a man. Better to be blurry and forgettable than to be memorable and meaningful. Better to be a drunken gnat in a urinal than to be the speculative identity of this whole universe. All of those expressed preferences are self-destructive and seem to rely on an abstract repudiation of some other person's idea of what it would be healthier to desire,

---

[18] In the newer version of this poem included in the Materials edition of Jeschke's poems, these two questions are replaced with a different one, in which the note of skepticism (perhaps intended in the first place to be self-directed) is somewhat diminished.

and I love them even for that, for being stupid and rebarbative, like people staggering out of a bar at night. They are the reminders I need throughout my own bouts of aphasia and cataplexy of the proximity of language to damage: both the true recognition of the ease with which solidarity with specific harm can fade out into silence or some other kind of hunger and the resurgence of historical intuition from within what seems like a total cognitive whiteout. It is ridiculous to write like this. I think that the poems make every shift and glitch in conscious purpose burn against the horizon of boring, infinite need, and that by this means and no other they illuminate the paths that a head fucked up by force of circumstance is able to take, on its way into a reality defined by class struggle, ageing, queues for food, the chain of events, conflicts over access to toilets, world wars, the drama of self-doubt banalized as virtue signaling, and everything else that drives us towards empty statements about how reality is complex and infinitely various. Poetry that knows this kind of wavering at the edge of speechlessness says all kinds of stupid shit. And it has to say it. And it has to say it because it knows that it is only by forcing language so close to need that it can be devoured by it that need becomes suddenly and acutely palpable.

These then are the two distinct impulses in *The Anthology*. The poetry says what it needs to in solidarity with what it can. It opposes and outgrows the art of plain transgressive impulsiveness under the pressure of this specific historical exigency, and it trains its attention exclusively on the language of what it needs and is presently denied. It is poetry that gives according to its abilities and that takes according to its needs. There are no good alternatives in it. For the faceless anti-eurocrats and chaise lounge generals, and for the paranoiacs waiting to see what the Stalinist emeritus says and for the Culture and Values humpers, and for the hordes of radical ambulance chasers who stalk about in the clouds of dust behind them, this won't be enough. And to all of these people the poetry has an answer, though it couldn't give a fuck whether it amounts to any kind of alternative or not; and the answer is the same one that we get in all genuine art of the rising class, from Rimbaud to Young MA, asserted with the same crude attention-grabbing, confetti-showering bang: *Rather be groped than marry "a man." Rather be forgettable than memorable. Rather be a gnat drunk on piss than some washed-up professor. And rather be coming up forever in a bad option than always coming down with a good one.*[19]

---

19 About 35 people turned out for Lisa's reading with Sam Solomon at the MayDay Rooms on Fleet Street on March 17, 2018. It had been a long winter and outside it was snowing heavily, the road more or less empty of the city workers who monopolize it on weekdays. Instead: buses, taxis, a smattering of drinkers wearing the St. Patrick's Day hats that you get given when you buy a pint Guinness. Glass-fronted office buildings, slush.

Lisa read her poems with an astonishing intensity. In a small room like the screening space in MayDay her projection is quite breathtaking: the poems are read loudly, unforgivingly; she gives them no space to recede or to breathe. She does not laugh at her own jokes or pause graciously to allow the puns to sink in. The effect is at once confrontational and generous. It is confrontational because it forces you to listen, squares up to you, dares you to keep sniggering. These are funny, weird texts, but their listener is given no opportunity to laugh them off. Lots of contemporary poetry readings establish a pact between author and reader in which each party acknowledges the intelligence of the other over the heads of the poems that are being read. Lisa's don't. As soon as one poem is finished, she slams the paper it was written on face down on the chair next to her and moves on to the next, only taking a breath to spit out the title. Her style is nervy, like a reader presenting their work for the first time: paper shaking, zero introduction, uncontrolled gestures even in front of an audience of comrades and friends. The nimbus of implied self-awareness that overshadows the poetry reading genre is burnt away by a really defiant sincerity, adopted in full awareness of the ridiculousness of some of the material that is being read and with a perverse and unyielding commitment to its (self-)defense. In some of the later poems this stance in delivery dovetails with a particular rhetoric of assertion: "I know that this sounds improbable but I *mean* it" (I am thinking of the new poem about public toilets being the most important form of infrastructure in contemporary society). And within this style of performance a narrow spectrum of tones, set off from one another very brilliantly by means of a practiced phrasing that seems to contradict, but which in fact just runs alongside of, the untrained adrenaline visible in wrists and neck and feet: "Eurotrash" read with horrific, wide-eyed gusto bordering on mania, the "song" in the middle fitted out with a nasty little tune. Intimations of immorality, fairground rides, carsickness, and stale beer. "The Future" a little slower and more deliberate, but only so as to ramp up the atmosphere of ill-fitting menace which had already seemed as if it might be getting out of hand.

Nowhere in this sequence a drop in the air pressure long-lasting enough for the mind to sink downwards into its second can of Stella. Generosity as well as confrontation pulses in this performance style because it identifies its performer with her language in all of its flare-ups of intractable candor; and it is generous towards its audience as well as towards the poems themselves because it doesn't try to lead it up the garden path of intelligent or knowing narcissism. I think everyone in the room could feel this and was grateful for it. At the end of Lisa's reading of her short poem in which she declares her love for Caster Semenya (a piece that in another setting might have seemed deliberately simplistic and childlike), there went up in the room a kind of deep murmur of assent. It was as if we had all seen what effort it cost her to stay within her language, and so could believe it when she broke out for a moment into one of its happiest and most familiar songs.

A video of the reading can be found here: MayDay Rooms, "Sam Solomon and Lisa Jeschke – Materials Poetry Reading Series," *YouTube*, March 18, 2018, https://www.youtube.com/watch?v=usAzYW1owdM&t=4s.

6

Poetry and Self-Defense: On Xu Lizhi and Nat Raha

《最后的墓地》
The Last Graveyard

Even the machine is nodding off
Sealed workshops store diseased iron
Wages concealed behind curtains
Like the love that young workers bury at the bottom of their hearts
With no time for expression, emotion crumbles into dust
They have stomachs forged of iron
Full of thick acid, sulfuric and nitric
Industry captures their tears before they have the chance to fall
Time flows by, their heads lost in fog
Output weighs down their age, pain works overtime day and night
In their lives, dizziness before their time is latent
The jig forces the skin to peel
And while it's at it, plates on a layer of aluminum alloy
Some still endure, while others are taken by illness
I am dozing between them, guarding
The last graveyard of our youth.

This is a poem by the poet Xu Lizhi, who three years after its composition killed himself by jumping from the seventeenth floor of a shopping mall in Shenzhen, to become one member of a small but historically significant group. The group was important enough for Steve Jobs to assert that it was statistically insignificant and threatening enough to impel Foxconn to raise employee wages by about twelve percent over a period of four years.[1] Like most groups that achieve their aims by some kind of collective action, nobody commented on the behavior of this one by describing it as "haunting" or "tragic" or as being "capable of opening a rare window" onto the experience of "the Chinese youth."[2] Nobody would have said this, nobody would have even conceived of such a response, because it was immediately obvious to anybody with eyes that the significance of the spate of Foxconn jumping suicides as a collective action was a total peremptory refusal of the conditions in which proletarian lives

---

1   Kathrin Hille, "Foxconn to Raise Salaries 20% after Suicides," *The Financial Times,* May 28, 2010, http://www.ft.com/cms/s/2/5e1ee750-6a05-11df-a978-00144feab49a.html. For some information about how the suicides galvanized other workers to participate in less self-destructive forms of struggle, see the article by the *Bloomberg* journalist Dexter Roberts, "The Rise of a Chinese Worker's Movement," *Bloomberg Weekly,* June 10, 2010. https://www.bloomberg.com/news/articles/2010-06-10/the-rise-of-a-chinese-workers-movement

. More general first-person reports on the recent history of Chinese factory labor can be found at the Gongchao website; Hao Ren, et al., "Factory Stories: On the Conditions and Struggles in Chinese Workplaces," *Gongchao.org,* 2012–2015, http://www.gongchao.org/en/factory-stories.

2   In order of appearance: Ishaan Tharoor, "The Haunting Poetry of a Chinese Factory Worker Who Committed Suicide," *The Washington Post,* November 12, 2014, https://www.washingtonpost.com/news/worldviews/wp/2014/11/12/the-haunting-poetry-of-a-chinese-factory-worker-who-committed-suicide/; Joshua Barrie, "Read the Heartbreaking Poems of a Man Who Committed Suicide After [*sic*] Working in a Foxconn Factory," *Business Insider UK,* November 6, 2014, http://uk.businessinsider.com/foxconn-factory-workers-suicide-poems-2014-11; Eva Dou, "After Suicide, Foxconn Worker's Poems Strike a Chord [*sic*]," *Wall Street Journal,* November 7, 2014, http://blogs.wsj.com/chinarealtime/2014/11/07/after-suicide-foxconn-workers-poems-strike-a-chord/.

are bought up for almost nothing and then made to stand for whatever their middle-class owners want them to.

None of these things were said about the group to which Xu Lizhi now unalterably belongs, but all of them were said about the poetry that Xu Lizhi wrote and which was translated and circulated in the months after his death. As soon as the first English-language translations of his poems were stolen, uncredited, from the communist labor activists who first produced them, to be re-posted to the *Bloomberg* website, a pernicious tendency was manifested in the vocabulary of critical description.³ For the journalist writing for the *Wall Street Journal,* Xu Lizhi was "a 24-year-old with literary aspirations." From this viewpoint, Xu Lizhi's poems were not "tragic" because they scream out for some responsive insight into a struggle against wretched social conditions, but because they are pathetic.⁴ The assertion that the poetry itself never does anything more than "open a window" onto or "offer a peek" at the circumstances that it contests insinuates that there isn't all that much to be seen.⁵ The poems

---

3   The original article and translations were by the group Nao. All of the materials can be found on the Libcom website: Nao, "The Poetry and Brief Life of a Foxconn Worker: Xu Lizhi (1990–2014)," *Libcom.org,* October 29, 2014, https://libcom.org/blog/xulizhi-foxconn-suicide-poetry. Everything in this chapter is stated in the spirit of gratitude to Nao for undertaking the work of translating these poems and for presenting them as they deserved to be presented.

4   Put from the perspective of its worst readers, the same point can be made differently. Poetry must be treated like this, as if it were the raw material for its own concept, and the intense and sustained labor of its human realization must be disregarded, because without this conceit it cannot be imagined as the symmetrically satisfying opposite of a concept of industrial labor. Working-class poets must be fobbed off with a vague desire for the idea of poetry and their actual accomplishments must be ignored, because otherwise their fate cannot be treated as if it were inevitable from the outset. The confrontation with actual poetry peremptorily disables this whole operation of moral response, since almost by definition actual poetry has nothing to do with predestination or with the sad acknowledgement of the necessary cruelty of whatever happens to be in the interests of the ruling classes in major Chinese export markets.

5   For "offer a peek," see Bendon Hong, "The Eerie Poetry of Chinese Suicide Victims [*sic*]," *Vice Online,* November 14, 2014, https://www.vice.com/

are "eerie," resonant; they symbolize the death of the person who wrote them, and make us think wistfully about what might have been ("literature"). I know of no more representative demonstration of the continued default association of poetry with middle-class values than the assumption that the main tragedy of Xu Lizhi's life was that he never had the chance to write poetry of a kind that middle-class authors can recognize, rather than the fact that he wrote powerful and accomplished poetry about the system from which they benefit and that that system ultimately killed him anyway.

Xu Lizhi's writing is of course traduced by this treatment and yet it seems defenseless in the face of it. Can it be defended? In the following short chapter, I will argue that it can be, and that, in spite of the liberties that business press journalists take with it, it can be defended principally because Xu Lizhi's poetry is itself an expressively defensive kind of writing. I also think that the character of its defensiveness, and the specific object that it chooses to defend, can tell us something useful about the history of capitalist violence and its present everyday extremities. Xu Lizhi's poetry may seem "tragic" to those for whom it suffers the conventionally tragic fatal flaw of being nothing but a vain striving towards an idea of poetry that it could never in fact attain, but my argument here is that the work belongs to another genre that is less recognized by institutional funding bodies and the lamenters of whatever might have been but now isn't. This is the genre of collective self-defense. In our present atmosphere of generalized disempowerment and habitual self-abnegation, this may not seem like a very plausible category for the description of poetry, especially since, according to the usual exclusionary logic, the phrase is more accurately used to describe self-organized food kitchens or rubbish collection or arms training. But Xu Lizhi's writing is itself the most lucid and exhaustingly definitive proof of the bankruptcy of that logic and of the self-attacking guilt that gives rise to it. It is clearly a very fundamental attempt to hold the self together by giving voice to some of

---

en_uk/read/death-poems-are-a-thing-in-china-right-now.

the tendencies that threaten to tear it apart, and the tone of the poetry is inseparable from its author's fundamental, desperate need for expressive control over the most basic dimensions of the situation that he was forced to confront. Defensive poetry is primarily defined by this characteristic, of exercising, and of working implacably to heighten, our expressive control over basic or fundamental experiences of capitalist violence, and also by the fact that it recognizes that this exercise of expressive control is a real and urgent collective and psychological need. Other bodies of work besides Xu Lizhi's can be used to show this — Xu Lizhi is in this respect only a singular and unforgettable case.

What defensiveness in language does *not* primarily involve is the prevention of misunderstanding. It is, much more importantly, a volatile and generous intuition of relative value. It begins in a basic recognition that something that is everything to you or to the people about whom you care is emphatically and unalterably nothing in the eyes of those who have control over the conditions in which you live. It is an immediate and bodily recognition of the insane violence of this historical relativity, which becomes more intense with every year in which the social distribution of produced wealth becomes more and more blatantly polarized. It is what makes a writer like Xu Lizhi say of his own expressive convictions that "[f]lowing through my veins, finally reaching the tip of my pen / Taking root in the paper / These words can be read only by the hearts of migrant workers." Or as someone else put it: "one is never obliged to speak the truth except in one's own language; in the enemy's language the lie must reign."[6] In other words, it is not an attempt to compel

---

6   Guy Debord, *Panegyric, Volumes 1 & 2*, trans. James McHale (London: Verso, 2004), 9. It is of course true that Xu Lizhi's statement that only migrant workers can understand his lines is different to Debord's assertion that one should only speak the truth in the language of the oppressed, since the second statement relies on the possibility of wilful obfuscation while the first does not. But there is still latent in Xu Lizhi's lines the idea that his poetry would be made into a lie once it was "translated" into the language of those who have no common feeling with migrant workers, and this is in fact demonstrably what did happen in the reporting of his poetry

those who rule over you to share your feelings but an attempt to induce in yourself a greater love for whatever it is whose value is capable of being reduced in their eyes to virtually nothing, so as to make of that reduction a still more maddeningly detestable and ridiculous emblem of the established and accepted cruelty of ordinary social life. It is a perverse and reactive attitude, bristling with pathological obstinacy, strung out in a feedback loop of self-harm and misrecognition. It is inseparable from love for that which is actually dominated, hurt, or broken, and at one of its extremes it can easily tip back into love for brokenness in and of itself. For the properly defensive writer, which is to say, for the writer who is habitually and attitudinally defensive, it is not only the case that what is everything for us is capable of becoming in the eyes of our enemy absolutely nothing, but that nothing can be anything except that which is liable at any moment to be reduced once again to nothing at all.

Defensive poetry has, besides this, two primary attributes or tendencies. The first of these has to do with magnification. The poetry springs from a recognition of the violence of relative value, but it does not follow from this fact that it is in any sense relativist or even yet, as a journalist for the *Wall Street Journal* might put it, that it has relativist "aspirations." It is not relativist; it is a total rejection of the fact that that which it values absolutely is even capable of being relativized. Everything and nothing become for the defensive poet like two distinct filters. All things are made to appear alternately under their different aspects, and the rhythm of the transformation sets the tempo for the protest it gives rise to. In Xu Lizhi's "The Last Graveyard," "The jig forces the skin to peel, / And while it's at it, plates on a layer of aluminum alloy." In the first line, my suffering is everything. In the second, it is nothing. Everything I am becomes greater under the light in which I appear as nothing at all, as the most immediately replaceable among an infinity of more valuable production factors, put to work until my skin blisters and

---

after his death. Defensiveness is what unites the two passages in spite of their different patterns of emphasis.

my body becomes unsuitable for the part-operation that it was employed to perform. It becomes inexorably greater under this light, because under it the possibility that everything I have and am and everything that I hope for will be violently taken from me is blown up and distorted and magnified until finally all of my horizons press in simultaneously on my life and squash it, densify it, jam it more and more relentlessly into just this moment of living expression cut off from the whole life in which we would never have to place on the former such demands as it could never hope to meet.

The second primary attribute of defensive poetry is that it is preemptive. Defensive poetry knows that it cannot have the whole life that it nevertheless wishes for. It wishes to empower its readers by confronting preemptively the violation that it realistically foresees for itself, by seeing more deeply and compassionately into its own brokenness and limitations and the constraints that are placed on its real and positive accomplishments than could any representative of the class who profit from these limitations and who write obituaries in which they call them a tragedy. "Most of us know," wrote Baraka in his poem "Das Kapital," that "there's a maniac loose. Our lives a jumble of frustrations / and unfilled / capacities."[7] And this knowledge is itself an excess capacity, however easy it may be to write down as empty aspiration or as negativity pure and simple. Middle-class critics think unfilled capacities are sad because they are incapable of ever being filled; defensive poets anticipate that response and are urged on by it, its negation of their lives, however exploited and needlessly damaged, is still the annihilation of everything that they have and wish to work with. They know instinctively and preemptively how to resist that response, and their poetry offers to it a humane and simple answer, by bringing forthrightly into view everything in the poet's life that breaks it up and steals the time of it—and they do so on the grounds that this

---

7   Amiri Baraka, "Das Kapital," in *Transbluesency: The Selected Poems of Amiri Baraka/LeRoi Jones (1961–1995)*, ed. Paul Vangelisti (New York: Marsilio Publishers, 1995), 153.

capacity to know the ways in which our capacities are unfilled is itself a real social power.

The excess of unfulfillment is a power. This is the slogan of the poetry of collective self-defense against the whimsical moralism of individual self-aggrandizement. Like all slogans, it is meant to condense an historical reality into a practical imperative, which is to say that it is meant to aid our thinking about how that reality might be exceeded. Capital abandons production and moves overseas, it leaves "the garbage cans parked full strewn / around our defaulting cities";[8] it then floods back into them in the form of private prison operators and other novel means of repression. Later it develops the technologies to allow whatever wealthy residents remain in de-industrialized zones to recruit workers to clear up their garbage but no one else's; it learns to profit from interactions that previously would have been too atomized for it to even notice.[9] All the while it succeeds overseas in liberating into its factories hundreds of millions of people who previously had been tied self-sustainingly to the land. How can this reality be exceeded? If historically the activity of self-defense has belonged mainly to those who are abandoned by capital — to those who are forced to struggle chiefly with its terroristic border guards, at the edges of states and in the centers of their largest conurbations — today the stakes have changed, and capital can now abandon you and take you up again several times even within the limits of an ordinarily curtailed lifetime. What does this mean for the political category of self-defense? And what does this mean for the language of self-defense, for defensiveness as a property of poetry intransigently committed to achieving a preemptive insight into the scale and the complexity of life that has been broken and cast off and fenced in and that still is not content to view itself as privatively under-privileged or merely evocatively dead?

---

8 Ibid.
9 See, e.g., PricewaterhouseCoopers, "The Sharing Economy," *Consumer Intelligence Series,* https://www.pwc.com/us/en/technology/publications/assets/pwc-consumer-intelligence-series-the-sharing-economy.pdf.

Some of these questions might be tested against the following lines by the poet Nat Raha:

> increasingly white bodies dispersed
>   early hours, new cross road:
> where we've held out in the try collective of us
> to construct a wedge ~~stable~~ , ~~of permanence~~ we
>   so broken out of belonging together
> root & rubble piling upon action to bruise, to be
>   thrown only back into privacy
>   / landlord behest::
>   sick w/ increase on values, the
>   suffering of our friends

This passage comes from "((a fire))," the first poem from a book titled *Of Sirens / Body & Faultlines*.[10] Raha has said of the zine format in which the poem was published that she wished the texts to "disappear"; this, I think, is another way of saying that she didn't desire the poems to possess any more permanence than the people who are constantly driven out by capitalist development in the city about which she writes. In any case, these are lines that die out freely and hotly on a border of neces-

---

10 Nat Raha, "((A fire))," in *Of Sirens / Body & Faultlines* (London: Veer Books, 2015), n.p. Raha provides the following primer on her blog: "as I said about the first edition—the pamphlet corresponds with 'radio / threat'. it was mostly written between summer 2014 and spring 2015 (with a few exceptions). trying to excavate and map sensations, discordances, the transformations of police reality and capital / canary wharf lookouts, moments of rupture in the locale of New Cross / Deptford in South London and beyond, of collectivity and protest, of what we are now calling radical transfeminism, of the constellations of violence that pivot around a government department known as the Home Office between the future and over 200 years before it was founded, of vague histories needing to be reclaimed and understood in the sense of understanding as a necessary synonym of decolonialization." See Nat Raha, "[Of Sirens / Body & Faultlines] Second Edition / Readings: Small Publishers Fair, Brighton with M. Nourbese Philip," *Sociopathetic Semaphores,* November 5, 2015, http://sociopatheticsemaphores.blogspot.com/2015/11/of-sirens-body-faultlines-second.html.

sitousness, which will go nowhere unfixedly, elaborating their brokenness as the substitute for abandonment and imposition. They are the push-factor for meaning that Baraka once sarcastically said was "self imposed": "the only thing worth living for," if being the only person alive is your kind of thing.[11] The words that get struck out in the fourth line are a joke about visibility: deletions highlighted in signal contrast to lives that are more silently extinguished, administratively shut out from the poem by the white bodies that fill it up in the "early hours" of the commuter shift. They are a kind of reading notes, as well as a muted commentary on the passive voice in which the first quoted line in this passage is constructed: a gloss for the grammar of ignorance is bliss.[12] More simply, they are an invitation to a closer and more sustained attention to what might here be the description of a squat eviction, or the breaking up of a shared home, of lives "thrown only back into privacy," which is the condition in which we are "so broken out of belonging together," each of these lines assembled out of the displaced prepositional rubble of the other, divided up by a self-commentary:

> so broken *back* belonging together
> root & rubble piling upon action to bruise, to be
> thrown only *out of* privacy

The yearning they express is for the process to be reversed, for it to be possible to go back, to belong together again, to be thrown out of the isolation that is irresistibly brought about by a political economy based in the inflationary monetization of basic human needs. The poem cries out for privacy and for association, mixes them up in "scenes of pollutant song" (n.p.); it shows us needs made contradictory by cramped proximity and also new ways to reverse their polarities. The "wedge" we tried to construct is denatured into a "we" and an "edge," then the "we" is

---

11 Baraka, "Gatsby's Theory of Aesthetics," *Transbluesency*, 132.
12 The point is that under current circumstances, white bodies are not "dispersed" but concentrated.

shunted out to the end of the line and is declassed into the edge that it was at first separated from. All the way across the jagged perimeter of this poetry and then out of and back into the heart of it, tenuous sense is left on display, scattered sensationally throughout the bits and pieces of descriptive vocabulary, tossed away or carelessly made to pile up against the "suffering of our friends," which is the one fact in these lines whose necessary recognition cannot be gotten clear from or broken down or made into a commentary on some text element that preceded it.

Defensive poetry sees preemptively into the fullest extent of the damage to which it is exposed. It recognizes in its detail a moving and communicative power, the use of which is not restricted to poetry but is the tenuous material of political connections that are still to be fleshed out in the reality that individually we get lost in. Raha's poetry indicates a historical qualification of this argument: the fullest extent of the damage to which we are now exposed has become intensely changeable, mobile, and dispersive, as capital has itself become changeable, mobile, and dispersive within and beyond the cities in which we live. Furthermore, as the points of connection and commonality between exploited and despairing people thousands of miles apart have multiplied, ramified, and grown together, they have begun to acquire a richer and more exacting language. This is the basis for a more substantive form of political mutuality.

How can this new mutuality be defended? It is easy to see how it might be destroyed, since the processes that threaten it are the same ones that bring it barely and incipiently into being. As capital expands into new areas of social life, it simultaneously abandons others. The kind of unfulfillment that has historically been created wherever money flees from a population is now expressed just as commonly in the political poetry of the contemporary Guangdong factory worker as in the work of the American poet-scholar. In this connection the description in Rosa Luxemburg's *The Accumulation of Capital* of the way in which capital accumulation is "primarily a relationship between capital and a non-capitalist environment" has never been more true.¹³ Her description of the process through which this "relationship" is established, by means of "[the] most complicated relations, divergences in the speed and direction of accumulation […] material and value relations with non-capitalist modes of production," has never been more exact.¹⁴ It becomes more formally exact not only because of its resistance to rigid formulae, but because of its expressive tone and style. Now, just as much as in 1972, Amiri Baraka's "jumble of frustrations and unfilled capacities" are the closest thing that we have in our internal lives to non-capitalist environments. They are blasts of fire in the consciousness of this morning, graveyards of a youth that we watch over with perverse contrariousness so as to know them more completely than our enemies who look over our shoulders. They are the essence of that deprivation that policymakers wistfully compassionate and that political poets like Xu Lizhi have preemptively defended, as a part of their life and experience, and they are the possibilities of a broken-down speech that in Raha's poems are pulled apart and put back together again at top speed in a blur of intelligent probation. They are all of these things and they are also historically changeable. In more recent poetry it becomes more and more clear that they are not stable fields of expressive dissatisfaction, in relation to which we have no obligation except to fortify their borders, since just at the point where they are felt most intensely they now split up, as Luxemburg predicted for political economy, into "the most complicated relations," and pass through perpetual divergences in the speed and direction of their accumulation: through forks in their relationship to their capitalist environment; through forward leaps and reverses in their potential expressive intensity; and more generally through all of the changes that might be expected to arise in a system of production whose growth and development has precisely nothing to do with human desire and satisfaction.

---

13   Rosa Luxemburg, *The Accumulation of Capital*, trans. Agnes Schwarzschild (London: Routledge, 2003), 398.
14   Ibid. The translation has been slightly adjusted.

What is most deeply characteristic of this vertiginous transformation is not anything so simplemindedly straightforward as an acceleration of existing social tendencies. It is a widening of the extremities within which historical struggles are formed and between which our jumble of frustrations and unfilled capacities are strung out. As more and more human beings are permitted to aspire to and also to achieve the kind of poetry that Xu Lizhi achieved so movingly, more and more people are faced with the threat that everything that they possess will be valued at and brutally reduced to nothing, on the basis that investment capital has been feeling a little down recently. Luxemburg's statement is important because she anticipated this historical transformation: because she knew that the defense of the excess of our unfulfillment would become for all proletarians more and more like a race across the entire surface of social need, and also that the surface is perpetually expanding, and that this can be true even with respect to the non-capitalist environments of a single human life. Luxemburg anticipated this transformation, and today Nat Raha produces poetry that is buffeted at the center of it, and until 2014 Xu Lizhi also lived through it, and ran headlong into it, and chased his own capacities right into the center of that propagandistic black hole into which non-capitalist environments are sucked only to be spat out again as slogans on employee wellbeing. They have titles like the Foxconn/Hon Hai *Social and Environmental Responsibility Report*,[15] and *Bloomberg* reports on them too.

Each of these writers provides a different point of access onto the same social reality. In this reality, which is the reality both of super-exploitation and of urban abandonment and penury, it is not only our ability to realize our desires, or clearly to express them, but even our ability to feel them that must be fought for and defended. *With no time for expression, emotion*

---

15 See, for instance, the Foxconn 2014 Social and Environmental Responsibility Report, covering the year of Xu Lizhi's death; Foxconn Technology Group, "2014 Social and Environmental Responsibility Report," June 2015, https://www.honhai.com/s3/reports/CSR%E5%A0%B1%E5%91%8A%E6%9B%B8/%E8%8B%B1%E6%96%87%E7%89%88/2014%20CSR%20report.pdf.

crumbles into dust. Each of the writers mentioned above shows us this and each of them shows us also that in poetry the fight cannot be won, that it can arrest but not halt the total liquidation of whatever vital powers we happen still to possess. Each of them shows us this, and yet each of them proves in spite of it a contrary position, which is that any new radical politics that would permit us to express our desires clearly or to realize them in practice will nevertheless be absolutely worthless until it can open itself up to the tones of those for whom even the capacity to feel can never be communicated except as a kind of fight to the death.[16] There will be no meaningful new radical politics that is incapable of speaking in the same tones as those for whom even the next breath is something that has to be defended at all costs. Those who now deny this proposition acquiesce to the violence of capitalist value and reduce to nothing a struggle that for many people has been everything that they could do to sustain themselves in the face of conditions that are absolutely inimical to any kind of life. Their way of reading is the normative way of reading. It mistakes proximity to death in desperate struggle for death itself, "tragic" and unavoidable.

And at the bottom of all of this there is a simple lesson. Anyone who chooses to listen to writing like Xu Lizhi's patiently and attentively engages in a fight against the violence of capitalist value and its forms of relativity. Those of us who are not Xu Lizhi's friends or comrades must choose to listen to his writing; we cannot be compelled to hear what goes on in it, since the poetry truly does lack even the most reduced capacity to fight back against those who would ignore it in a fit of condescen-

---

16 As another writer who knew pretty well about this logic put it: "The man who has never received a kind message, a gesture, and who has never held anything of value, material or otherwise, if he is healthy, or I should say remains healthy (my persuasion presupposes original innocence), he never becomes so practical as to expect more of the same — nothing. Less but never nothing.

"To be denied or rejected means less to this man but never nothing." See George Jackson, *Soledad Brother: The Prison Letters of George Jackson* (Chicago: Lawrence Hill Books, 1994), 321.

sion. Nothing that Xu Lizhi has done or that anyone else will ever do will ever be able to compel understanding of the writing in those who are determined to hear in it nothing but the tragic absence of the poetry that they presume workers are incapable of writing. And yet, anyone who goes on treating the writing as if it were nothing will one day come in for a horribly nasty surprise.

Afterword: From a Letter to Some Friends

… I am not very happy with the essay that I sent to you both, I have rewritten it several times already. It still lacks to my eyes any clear sense of internal purpose. It is neither really an essay about Xu Lizhi nor an essay about self-defense.

What I most wanted to do is to write an essay about a particular kind of tone. It is obvious to me that tonal particularity in poetry — and not just in poetry — is a product of basic psychological disposition. Psychology is the base to poetry's tonal superstructure. The expressive range that is available in any kind of writing that cares about things like "expressive range" is predetermined to a substantial extent by the attitudinal habits of the writer. If the writer mostly thinks about social suffering by processing articles on the internet (the psychology of compulsive indigestion), then the tonal contour that they are most likely to be able to access is a tone of sublime horror. Their writing will be irresistibly controlled by this primary experience, of watching something unimaginably large and complex drip torturously through one uselessly constricting but also unsealable aperture, the drive-in window repurposed into a bilge pipe. Different writers will be able to express this basic psychological habitus with different degrees of ferocity or bland complacency, depending on who they are and how much they get paid for being it; and some of them will be able to manipulate the tone to which it gives rise with great and impressive facility; and some of them will be able to drive it towards its further limits of intensity; and some of them will be able to learn from it right up to its outermost accession; but the tone is still basically the same regardless. I am not putting this very well. I mean, I suppose, that the very best writer in this line is likely to throw all of their energies into the task of heightening and of accenting and of speeding up the basic psychological experience of digitally processing the data of contemporary social misery. If the basic experience is inattentive, twitchy, trigger-happy on a trackpad, then what poetry will do is work up that basic experience into a riot of expressive confusion. Out of the everyday experience of getting waylaid on a historical learning curve and dragged off by an impulse to the virtual clothes store, it will discount the whole universe by 50 percent. Out of the experience of not knowing what to click on next, it will user-generate a more totally hyperventilated parataxis. The tone is overwhelming and luxurious and seductive, but it is still a translation of the same old familiar mental bad habits, unaltered by being built out into an OCD megamall crisscrossed by overused conjunctions.

In the face of this kind of work it is not adequate to say that it is necessary to produce better writing. Some of this writing may be deliriously good as a translation of the basic psychological attitude from which it results, but this is like saying that the military junta in Egypt is deliriously good as a translation of the Mubarak regime of 2009. It is not the deluxe intensification of the attitude that needs changing, but the attitude itself. It is a precondition for poetry that its authors learn to rip out of their heads the affirmative tendency to treat suffering as if it were most conspicuously sublimely excessive and horrible. The cultivation of this basic attitude involves wasting expressive energy not on overcoming a social and political limitation, but on making that limitation strange and impetuously seductive. With every new accomplishment in the extreme intensification of the tone that is associated with this mental habit, which is in its everyday form unutterably tedious and banal, poets bring about a new reason to believe that the attitude is intrinsically worthwhile and defensible. By throwing all of their powers of invention and originality into the service of upcycling and tonally dynamizing the basic attitude I am describing, they reproduce in their audiences the conviction that, because their basic mental habits can be expressed intensely, there is no reason for those habits to be denied or refuted or overcome. The negative outcome of this conviction is that poetry can become more and more tonally explosive and far-out even as it makes other and more humane and fierce and politically desirable attitudes progressively less and less possible, both for its authors and its readers. The constant tonal dynamizing of attitudes of spectatorial horror makes it more and more evidently impossible to imagine that any other attitude could ever be brought to expression with the same kind of impetuous force. This makes poetry progressively less interesting, even as it becomes more inescapable.

I say all this to set up some background for a quite different kind of response. Xu Lizhi's writing had the effect on me that it did because it shocked me into a recognition of the fact that there are other attitudes towards which contemporary poets might feel instinctively and powerfully drawn. The tone of his writing seems to me as if it is in some very direct and straightforward sense the opposite of the tone of the work I am describing above. It is a fiercely defensive tone, because it recognizes on the basis of lived necessity the need to hang on to every moment of expressive potential, however compromised by exhaustion or despair. The tone is expressive of a personality that cannot afford to find suffering sublimely excessive, and that needs to hold onto and defend really whatever it can. Often the tone of the work cannot be driven to excess and the poems give conscious voice to this fact: they just have to happen anyway, and more than that they *just have* to happen, because if they don't then there is nothing else and because any increment of life that can be won against that eventuality is everything to the person who knows how close they are to finding life absolutely unlivable. It is meaningless to talk about whether they are "good" or "bad" poems, they are a lesson in something that from the perspective of the writers of the most sublimely blocked-up and spectatorially horrified poetry will simply seem unthinkable. The attitude that they evince is completely foreign to anyone who has become accustomed to the idea that the suffering of an individual cannot be expressively conceived otherwise than as a spectacular case of injustice that then stands in for a million other cases of cruelty that all belong under the same heading. I don't think that we know, in our present situation, what it would sound like if anyone or if a large group of English-language writers, a movement or a collective, were to achieve by some effort of sustained commitment or will a real and practical insight into the basic attitude of Xu Lizhi's writing. I don't think that we know what it would sound like if that attitude were suddenly to punch its way through into the tone of the poetry that the candidate-writers are now composing. I don't think we know how that would feel. So I have no idea at all what it would mean for more writers to learn not only to adopt the attitude of defensiveness that we can find in Xu Lizhi, but also to do with it just what has been done for the basic attitude of spectatorial horror and sublime impotence that is now the most tonally elaborated and outspoken and dynamized basic attitude in the culture. I have no idea what it would be like if there were to surge into the world a poetry whose attitude of careful and defensive commitment to the real lives of suffering and exploited individuals were also as freely elaborated and dynamized as that. But I do think that a writing like this might help people to live instead of annually upgrading their experience of failing to do so.

7

Wound Building: On T.S. Eliot, Amiri Baraka, Bernadette Mayer, and Keston Sutherland

> *Yes. Being unemployed and without food can make you very sad.*
> — Jayne Cortez[1]

I feel that perhaps it's possible to begin to summarize. Many of the chapters in this book have been about trying to feel something. They are about feelings that it is difficult, rather than impossible not, to have. The earliest of these pieces talk about this problem in the language of psychoanalysis: the theory of mental processes that underlie our experiences of numbness, speechlessness or, in the technical sense of the word, apathy. I now want to talk about it in the language of being unemployed and without food, in a council flat in Nottingham in June 2018.

I treat poetry like a magnifying glass. I put my ideas under it and they burn up like ants. I understand that this may seem sadistic, but it is the largeness of the ideas that is unbearable to me. Errol Graham weighed four-and-a-half stone (30kg) when his body was found by bailiffs who broke into his Nottingham

---

[1] "Supersurrealist Vision: Interview with Jayne Cortez," in *Heroism in the New Black Poetry: Introductions and Interviews,* ed. D.H. Melhem (Lexington: University of Kentuck, 1990), 201.

council flat to evict him. He had become unendurably small. So this is how it will be. No arms / exist for me, but those locked in doors, and indoors, with and without a space, across all distance, forever. I cannot separate this from a thought about love poetry, and this is fucking disgusting to me; and I still cannot do it.

The first draft of this chapter was about immediacy. I felt like I had been suffocated by my ideas, and that I needed to learn to talk about whatever was right in front of me. I had come to feel, obscurely, that my inability to value particulars in poetry was related to my inability to talk about my feelings in life, other than in the register of florid political despair in which I had become native, and I wanted to change that state of affairs, to alter the one through the other. Also, I wanted to know in what sense the immediacy that I desired was a placebo, a commodity, and an illusion, at a time when what you might call *idiomatic* immediacy, the symbolically codified immediacy of damaging intoxication — of pain — had become so widely transacted in the mainstream culture as to be effectively its dominant mode. As a Marxist I still feel a residual desire to explain this. I look out my window. The sky is like a magnifying glass.

Two years and many distractions later, and some things have begun to feel clearer. I hate big ideas; lyric poetry continues to be one of the ways in which we talk about how we're sick-n-tired of them. We write lyrics to say "fuck you" to our thoughts, to their vagueness and powerlessness and fixity, and to the way that we see them repeat themselves unchangingly throughout our lives and all of their reverses. I owe this particular formulation of the problem to the poet Jack Frost; the basic disposition I owe to almost every contemporary writer who I am able to feel passionate about. To damage and reduce the world through the medium of our idea of it is one of the ways we learn to love what is in front of us without any debilitating sense of proportion. This is what I think of my own big ideas:

> I told the archeologist that I would've
> liked to be able to represent my culture
>   — dead or alive — without any suffering,
> but if I'm insolent and wonderless
> it's cause I'm fucking sick-n-tired
> of the imperative to ruthlessness
> that I endure to court your ruthlessness.
> and if I choose this ruthlessness
> it's in order to prevail against you,
> you, the specialists on whose lips
> I live as something I can barely recognize
> and to hope that in each act
> of meanness against you
> that what prevails begins now —
> in rattlesnakes and watersnakes
> and gardensnakes and graveyards
> and water graves.[2]

The poets I will discuss in what follows are T.S. Eliot, Amiri Baraka, Bernadette Mayer, and Keston Sutherland. These poets don't share any particular relation to immediacy or direct speech. Any attempt to construct a history of those things with exclusive reference to their work would be ridiculous. I am just trying to get some elements of a problem into view.

·

Here is a famous, early instance of what I just called idiomatic immediacy:

> Let us go, through certain half-deserted streets,
> The muttering retreats
> Of restless nights in one-night cheap hotels

---

[2] Jackqueline Frost, *The Third Event: Part Three* (London: Crater, 2019), 15. This book accompanies *The Third Event: Part 1 & 2* (Cambridge: Tipped Press, 2018).

> And sawdust restaurants with oyster-shells [...][3]

These stupid, trivial lines by T.S. Eliot are the sound of a resignation so rehearsed that it hurts to listen to it. The first words are a command only slightly concealed by the expression of mutuality: *Let us go — let go — give up*. The street that may as well be any other is what we give ourselves up into; it is the common architecture that is half-full of people or full of half-people, indifferent in the tepid half-light of half-generic, only ever half-serious anomie, the halved promise of self-harm that might help us at least to forget the hurt that it increases by attenuation, like the sounds of the word *hurt* eked out across "*h*al*f*-des*er*ted," etherized into an aesthetic that 107 years later still thrives in the fake immediacy of "streets." The whole music of the verses serves the purpose of strengthening this argument by means of practiced imprecision. It tells us to let go not only of ourselves but of the definition of our objects also, as the rhyme of "certain" and "deserted" makes these two quite contrary words collapse into the general credo of resignation: Let go of whatever you might have known for certain, since knowledge is a desert; let go of the specificity of social institutions, since the people who make them are stunted and unreal; and let go of mutuality too, of *us*, let *us* go, by letting go of the idea of a society whose streets and homes might be a source of material and not a symbol of vacuity.

The interchangeability of those last two terms is so insidiously central to our culture that it can feel difficult to express. It involves more than the degradation of the world into a symbol of interior experience, the concealment of narcissistic withdrawal as a withdrawal into reality, in the form of the cheap hotels and minicab kiosks that proliferate in these settings. And it involves more than this because it also models the shrinking of reality: the definite, relentless sensation of the narrowing of the world

---

3   T.S. Eliot, "The Love Song of J. Alfred Prufrock," in *Collected Poems, 1909–1962* (New York: Harcourt, Brace & World, 1963), 3.

to the scale of the personal disaster that blots it out, in a court proceeding or debt relation or cell.

Eliot could enjoy this transformation of reality into the symbol of its vacuity because of who he was. The idiom of his early poetry makes the real, concrete, daily world seem as filmy and unreal as a mirror reflecting on itself: an empty geometrical cube by any other name. This method of description is made more poignant still by the suggestion, really no more than a kind of atmosphere, of a parity of hurt between the person who "lets go" of himself in this reality, and the person who it has taken hold of with the force of an iron vise. Its candidacy as a dominant idiom is premised on this atmosphere of equivalence, just as the dominance of a capitalist political party is premised on its pretense of speaking in the general interest. Anyone can become a member of reality shrinking or fading, can smell some aspect of their private experience hanging in the stairwells of it. Anyone can do anything in it to anyone and through the haze of non-specific trauma that it enfolds can feel in themselves the sexual license of a responsibility that has become all at once beautifully diminished.

What do we gain from staying in this idiom, and what do we lose? How many ways are there of being in it, and how has it changed across the century in which it first emerged, as the expressive innovation of a handful of overeducated Christian bankers? If the idiom mystifies class reality by providing a language in which all hurt dissolves into an atmosphere of convenient parity, and yet remains at the same time the dominant form in which the daily realities of our concrete historical society and its institutions are inventoried and processed, what use is it, or can it be?

> Smoke seeping from my veins. Loss from
> the eyes. Seeing winter throw its wind
> around. Hoping for more, than I'll ever

have.[4]

This example of the idiom, dating from the mid-twentieth century, changes the kind of self-consciousness with which Eliot first introduced it. While "The Love Song of J. Alfred Prufrock" delectates in self-consciousness of the world reduced to a symbol, Amiri Baraka's poem is full of feelings of hostility towards it: a street punctuated with the intestines of financiers and snow, drifting home silently, holding the steering wheel of the car and staring out into the limits of control, in dumb recognition of the fact that the power to manipulate one part of the world can only accentuate our feelings of powerlessness in another. "[M]ore, than I'll ever / have." A prize for this realization.[5] But the lines are also about carelessness. The season that throws its wind around is slapdash, unfocused; it wastes its own resources or expends them prodigiously and without circumspection. Perhaps it expresses also our own carelessness: the ways in which we aren't looking after ourselves, the intuition that our commitment to working, living, writing, etc., takes a toll on us, causing our organs to drift around in our bodies listlessly and to slump in their cavities, like drunks making their ways towards the back of the bar at midmorning, barely remembering to pump or suck. Baraka also writes about this at the beginning — he is a master of beginnings — of his "Letter to E. Franklin Frazier," his poem addressed to the African American sociologist who was responsible for the first serious historical criticism of the US Black middle class in the high era of post-war conformism:

---

[4] Amiri Baraka, "The Burning General," in *Transbluesency: The Selected Poems of Amiri Baraka/LeRoi Jones (1961–1995)*, ed. Paul Vangelisti (New York: Marsilio Publishers, 1995), 129.

[5] I think that Baraka saw this in his writing, which is why descriptions like the one that I just quoted become increasingly scarce in his work from the mid-1960s onwards, and are replaced more and more frequently with arguments in a different register: "a real world breathing — inhaling exhaling concrete & sand" (165); a world whose reality is defined not by the brilliant artificiality of our descriptions of it, but by the violence of the emphasis with which I am willing to insist that it is there to be lived in, in spite of the "capitalist flunky film hacks" (163) who buy it up.

> Those days when it was all right
> to be a criminal, or die, a postman's son,
> full of hallways and garbage, behind the hotdog store
> or in the parking lots of the beautiful beer factory[6]

To die full of hallways and garbage. The construction here is as negligent as the world that throws us around: a glaring ellipsis in grammar held together by precise symmetries in phonology, whose promise that it was al*right* to *die* be*hind* the hotdog store — long vowels creating a virtual refrain, for it was alright to die behind the hotdog store — eventually makes everything else sound totally irrelevant. It *is* alright to die behind the hotdog store: the effort expended on making it so renders carelessness inaudible, even when it fills our corpses with hallways and garbage or makes our selves that are not yet corpses into "a jumble of frustrations and unfilled / capacities," as it must.[7] Baraka had as much reason as anyone to hate Eliot, and his early work, from the period in which he was developing his cultural nationalism, is everywhere full of registrations of this specific intellectual struggle: "Who is T.S. Eliot? So what? A cross."[8] His later turn against the Eliotian idiom remains perhaps the greatest single instance of a rejection of everything that that idiom stands for or can be made to represent: a new music of the populated streets, conceived in explicitly Marxist terms. And yet the idiom

---

[6] Baraka, "Letter to E. Franklin Frazier," in *Transbluesency*, 121.

[7] To use the vocabulary that Baraka would adopt slightly later in his writing: Baraka, "Das Kapital," in *Transbluesency*, 151. The metaphors remain faithful to Baraka's earlier instincts. "Our lives" are a symbolic vacant space just as the winter was when it threw its winds around.

[8] Amiri Baraka [Leroi Jones], *The System of Dante's Hell: A Novel* (New York: Grove Press, 1966), 134. Getting beyond T.S. Eliot was a consistent preoccupation of black writers in the US fighting for a new idiom in the 1960s and early '70s: his name was a synecdoche for the symbolic literary misuse of the "half-deserted streets" that many African American poets grew up in. See Ishmael Reed, "Badman of the Guest Professor," in *Every Goodbye Ain't Gone: An Anthology of Innovative Poetry by African Americans,* eds. Aldon Lynn Neilson and Lauri Ramey (Tuscaloosa: University of Alabama Press, 2006).

has continued to develop irresistibly. It has grown wildly and profligately beyond the limits of any particular middle-class anomie, and now works its way outwards into the rhythms of contemporary music and the whole atmosphere of the mass culture to which it might once have seemed diametrically opposed. Other, quite different poets have seen another side of the same problem. When in her *Sonnets* Bernadette Mayer wrote that "It might be right to write of just the hour / That's a structure good as love's or any measure," she transferred the central problem of New York school immediacy into an antithetical vocabulary of structures and systems:

> And young he (there's always been this dare) sleeps waking
> Partly sideways, mollescent yet macho (only joking)
> Always retreating back to what the lawned home
> Or something irreligious might be, who knows what's known?
> Many other absent things done in times like ours of these
> Unfulfill love's presence like it was one of those
> Displayed wedding cakes on 14th street with a bed of pink
> Beside the hockey players, if you begin young to think
> Life is shit you're better off later when you get
> A sort of basketballish hope from your fancier genes yet
> I've seen how the light looks in each circumstance
> And gone out to get oranges, Tide and water all at once
>
> It might be right to write of just the hour
> That's a structure good as love's or any measure

The gesture is distinctive and historically singular.[9] Frank O'Hara had also written of "just the hour," as anyone who has ever read any of his poems will know. His whole reputation in

---

9 Bernadette Mayer, "Spooky Action from a Distance: Sonnet About How Love Is as Teaching as You Breathe Deeply with Disrespect for the Text and Become Disjecta Membra from Your Lover," in *Sonnets* (New York: Tender Buttons Press, 2014), 72.

post-war American poetry hangs on this particular innovation.[10] But he had not recognized the hour as "a structure," as if it were a building or a prison; and in fact Mayer herself seems to shrink from the formulation even as she advances it. The auxiliary verb muscles in on the proposition at its very beginning, in a chain of trivial rhymes ("might," "right," "write"), and in the second line the assertion trails off into near incoherence: is "love" a structure? is it a "measure" like any other? why would I even want to try to answer these questions? The uncertainties accumulate in the back of the reader's mind until the statement around which they proliferate seems to fold under the weight of them, like a tarpaulin under heavy rain, and the lines begin to suggest themselves as meaningless or deliberately incoherent or self-sabotaging. But the solidity of the couplet just about holds the proposition up. And so the question survives: In what sense could we think of an hour as a structure? Why might that formulation be appealing, not just as an attempt to open up poetry to the fullest possible range of experience, in the same burst of metropolitan post-war optimism that made it "all right" to die behind a hotdog store, but as a gesture of psychic defensiveness?

> Now older than we were before we were forty
> And working so much in an owned world for rent money
> Where there seems little time for the ancient hilarity[11]

I think that Mayer's writing from this period about the way that wage labor and landlordism pulverize our imaginative and sexual lives is all about immediacy in the specific sense of world-diminution; and her thinking is antithetical to Eliot's because she is so brilliantly determined to ensure that if she is compelled to live out her experience on a smaller scale than the one that she might freely choose, then she will make this compulsion her own. The structure of the hour will be a structure possessed of its own dynamics and laws and its own political economy, and

---

10 Frank O'Hara, *Lunch Poems* (San Francisco: City Lights Books, 2014).
11 Mayer, "Birthday Sonnet for Grace," in *Sonnets*, 52.

its own descents into nihilism and its own resurgence back out into the self-assurance that we cannot hold onto, when from hour to hour we find ourselves in the grip of a belief that "structure" is something that always happens elsewhere. This is what the poetic structure of *the* hour might be, why it might be as good as love's structure, the measure of our ability to pull ourselves together.

It might be possible now to take a step back. When I reduce the world, what is it that I want to achieve? Do I want (a) to make it malleable, so as the better to intervene in it; (b) to dramatize the carelessness with which I treat myself, so that my habits of self-harm are externalized into the amputated environments that I pretend to describe; (c) to romanticize the movement out of ideology and into some stage-set of faked immediacy; or (d) to preserve it at the scale at which I can hope to give it structure? Could this grid, the terms of which might be described, crudely, as Brechtian, Barakian, Eliotian, and Mayerian respectively, provide one way of approaching the history of what is now the dominant idiom? In my own thinking I feel the pull of all of these terms, and in fact they are closer to my instincts than almost any other literary effects that I can now think of, although some of the terms I despise and want to reject, while others seem to me like things to be getting on with. In any case, could this grid make the politics of representatively damaged or reduced worlds easier to assess? Could it help us to think about what it means to write right now, in this present, against the enormously elaborated and intoxicating expressive culture of individual hurt, woundedness, isolation?

The dominant idiom first emerged into English poetry as a mere backdrop to intellectual disillusionment, a burlesque of downward mobility serving the higher purpose of an existential crisis. The crisis took place always at the level of ideas. In some poetry of the mid-twentieth century, the idiom was transformed into a way of describing the pain of wanting to get back into a concrete social reality, into a popular life that remains unwelcoming, alienating, hurtful, or unreal. By the 1980s, at the time that Mayer was working, its increasing pressure in the larger culture meant that it could feel like a "structure": finding oneself overwhelmed by immediacy, unable to think ahead, fucked up at work or in the constant scramble to pay the rent, traumatized sexually or by the thickness of despondency, and watching on helplessly as the most mundane daily tasks expand into unsurpassable obstacles, comes to feel not like the opposite of what we might call structural thinking, but its very substance. It is our only structure — as good as love's or any other measure — and it flows outwards from here into the common sense of the popular culture. Finally, it becomes the space in which certain kinds of atmospheric pleasure become uniquely available to us, if only we are willing to immerse ourselves in it.

The dominant idiom is the idiom of a world reduced to concrete immediacy by trauma. It is flexible enough to convey the real experiences of class oppression, the richest expressions of relief, and the most inert justifications for exploitation, abuse, and institutional oppression. Experiencing happiness, love, or comradeship, we reach through this idiom as if through an empty geometrical space, and the reality that we stretch out towards recedes and goes dim like in any generic depiction of drowning. How we can come up from this structure, how we can kick our way back out of the fishbowls of ourselves, like stock characters in a cheap TV drama, sliding naked in a sheen of patience back into the reality of disanaesthesia, is a question we have barely started to ask. The remaining part of this essay is an attempt barely to ask it: to describe what it feels like, now, to become immersed in the dominant idiom, in the effort to arrive on the other side of it. It will focus, primarily, on the recent poetry of Keston Sutherland, where the structure of this expressive situation is treated more literally than in any other body of work that I know.

•

Here is a passage of Keston's poetry that I think of in this connection:

> slowly the park is colourless
>   it should become that
> re-entered way, not and of to begin
>   with more to begin with you
> should hear say a bent put by, no way were that what just
>   inside its own stayed
> flare you'll ask to freeze, high vacuum
>   conditioning to a crass jot in
> rate-saccharine stop how stop how put
>   by does her
> the park is flashing does
>   her[12]

These are some lines from near to the beginning of Keston Sutherland's very early poem "Mincemeat Seesaw." They re-enter a topos that earlier poets had already explored very thoroughly: the functionalized landscape — here "the park," a once aristocratic, now municipal environment, landscaped and controlled by curfew, and made to stand by virtue of a long history of state paternalism for the public who are alleged to be its beneficiaries — that is first made to exteriorize a feeling of isolation ("slowly the park is colourless"), then made to ridicule exactly that ("the park is flashing"). The main formal discovery of the work is particular to its monosyllables ("not and of to begin / with more to begin with you") and the pressurized stuttering they create: noise of a head buffeted by doubt or self-accusation; the sparking and bursting of particles that serve as trailers for an utterance that remains forever on the cutting-room floor.

In terms of the grid I set out earlier, the crudeness of this language is of type (b), with a little bit of (c) sprinkled in for good measure. Type (b), because the language is full of climactic displays of self-neglect. Its scene is a flare you'll ask to freeze "just / inside": intimations of a homelessness that is real and not metaphysical. Also real is the despair that makes harm

---

12 Keston Sutherland, "Mincemeat Seesaw," in *Poetical Works 1999–2015* (London: Enitharmon Press, 2015), 48.

something partly invited, even when it is also violently imposed: "you'll ask [the flare] / to freeze." But the language belongs to type (c) because the world it presents is deliberately reduced. It is a toy park, as unreal as any "one-night cheap hotel." It is a social object very consciously reduced to a symbol, and then made slowly to black out and glitter so as to advertise that transformation, and to shine garishly like a head kicked in before at last it pops and vomits meaninglessly. A "crass jot." Birdsong. Whether the conversion of the real world into an atmospheric effect is best attacked like this is an outstanding question for Keston Sutherland's own poetry, and the black hole of low amplitude into which social facts are sucked and condensed into "moods" is vandalized differently in his later work, if never with as much volatile ambivalence as here, in this early merry-go-round of broken anaphora, and beneath the fog of just these relative pronouns. But by the same token I know of no other poetry that is so preoccupied with the construction *and dissolution* of symbols, or that takes the congelation of immediacies in language so seriously. What screams for overwhelming immediacy in one moment is at the next nothing except cops farting in a clearing. This is why when the park flashes and blows its fuse it conveys almost in spite of itself the promise, if not the total reality, of the first type of crudeness that I am trying to specify, of world-reduction, type (a): the preoccupation with the transformation of complex social reality into something brick-like and manipulable, as memorably reductive as the *Communist Manifesto,* and now focused specifically on the experience of immersion itself, conceived as a topos, or idiom.

Why would we abandon that promise? Other contemporary poets have written work more recently that has dealt with this problem in different ways and from different perspectives. Timothy Thornton and Ian Heames have written poetry in which the idiom is thematized with variant obsessiveness; Simone White has written about (and also into) its place in recent rap; Diane Hamilton and Porpentine Charity Heartscape have featured in or made computer games that simulate it.[13] In 2015 Thornton published a book of poems with the title *Water and Burning Effects On/Off*, which expresses with the beautiful, surprising abruptness of the best of his writing both the desire to be able to accomplish this kind of immersiveness and the impetuous, frantic urge to snap out of it. All this is just another way of saying that exposure to half-desertedness, how Eliot wanted the world to be, is right now anyone's head's default setting. And what is sometimes called the "transitional" quality of the period is just the reflex of that same instinct, forcing us into the exile of some unspecified future, to breathe in an atmosphere of sci-fi idiolects, in the precincts of its own stayed flare.Perhaps because of this, Keston Sutherland's poetry has for several years conducted a kind of running argument with immersiveness. In his *Odes to the TL61P* he writes, with a self-attacking instinct completely unaltered by the switch in register, that "poetry evolves from a vivid play of nerves and confusions into sedative aporiae in mock-heroic marginalese, if you don't take precautions to prevent it,"[14] identifying with what to me seems like an almost impossibly, woundingly stiff piece of self-conscious notation, like in a diary entry, the disappearance from his writing of most of the verbal effects that had first characterized it. In the same poem, the symbols of a shrunken world that denote simulated

---

13 See Timothy Thornton, *Water and Burning Effects On/Off* (Cambridge: Shit Valley, 2015); virtually the entire corpus of Ian Heames, but especially his physically inaccessible series of Sonnets, reviewed by David Grundy in his "'As Life is to Other Themes': Ian Heames' *Sonnets*," *Streams of Expression*, September 9, 2015, http://streamsofexpression.blogspot.com/2015/09/as-life-is-to-other-themes-ian-heames.html; Simone White's writing on the role of the "grid" of black expression in the music of Vince Staples, in her essay "Dear Angel of Death," published with her poetry in *Dear Angel of Death* (New York: Ugly Duckling Presse, 2018); Alejandro Miguel Justino Crawford's *Diana Hamilton's Dreams* (Oakland: Gauss PDF, 2016), https://gausspdf.itch.io/dhd; and Porpentine Charity Heartscape, *Everything You Swallow Will One Day Come Up Like a Stone,* available via Amanda Wallace, "Twine: Everything You Swallow Will One Day Come Up Like a Stone," *Storycade,* 2014, http://storycade.com/twine-everything-swallow-will-one-day-come-like-stone/.

14 Sutherland, *The Odes to the TL61P*, in *Poetical Works*, 331.

immediacy (Eliotian immediacy) appear exclusively in scenes of sexual memory, in arch, moderately pathetic descriptions of "a wire fence threaded at random but distractedly with abstractions of childish plants and weeds, after school"[15] (see also the mount "I go on to" where "[i]t is snowing a bit").[16] But does that adequately answer the question? Does poetry "evolve" out of the immersiveness — the reduced world, scene of nervous "confusions" — in which it begins? If it does, most poets writing now about their own fucking lives, instead of frantically trying to cover them up, are stuck in some kind of perpetual immaturity. Are they?

It seems to me that this evolutionary hypothesis in Keston Sutherland's poetry is at least in part self-attacking. It also runs up against a counterclaim, a commitment that intrudes more deeply into his writing, and which his work shares with other poets as various as John Keats, Jayne Cortez, and Lisa Jeschke. The counterhypothesis is more or less as follows. The correct response to Eliotian fantasies of a deserted world is not to give up on immediacy altogether, or to grow out of it and into meditative prosaic expansiveness, but to fill the world up. Poetry fills.[17] This is its formal and political destiny. It struggles against Eliotian immediacy by an equal and opposite effort of literal projection: into the dark night, the quiet clearings, the exquisite trap, "the hour" that we have left over, the aesthetic forms that it is good manners to leave half empty, the blanks and fissures of performed depression, all of it, the pauses and pregnant silences

---

15   Ibid., 340.
16   Ibid., 353.
17   Sutherland has written about this, at great length and in a number of different contexts, and this whole essay is in part an attempt to approach his terms from a slightly different angle. Starting points are his lecture "Blocks: Form Since the Crash — A Seminar at New York University, 13 November 2015," available via Internet Archive, https://archive.org/details/BlocksSeminarAtNYU13November2015, and his remarks in "Keston Sutherland & John Tamplin: Transcription of a Conversation in Princeton, U.S.A., 7th December 2015," ("crushing life down with my forehead into a tube"), *Black Box Manifold* 17 (Winter 2016), http://www.manifold.group.shef.ac.uk/issue17/KestonSutherlandJohnTamplinBM17.html.

and the "[s]quare snow" that we pencil into them,[18] the prudent omissions and excisions, constantly, into all of them, it projects its life and its substance until they swim with it:

> Ritual fart
> and navel of rebellious stink
> urination and energetic repulsion
> poetic orgasm and guttural belch of erotic storm
> let your dynamism grunt[19]

These lines from Cortez's elegy for Larry Neale are a spoken challenge to the idea that poetry is something that we should be immersed in and not something that flows back out into the world. It has a feeling, but this feeling is not the kind of which we could say that it intimates some emergent truth that is as yet unavailable to cognition.[20] The poem knows what it feels and

---

18 "The snow was / even and undisturbed as we fingered / the tungsten evaporation boats and screamed shit. / Square snow blackened by manic recitative" (Sutherland, "Hot White Andy," in *Poetical Works*, 217).

19 Jayne Cortez, "No Simple Explanations (To the Memory of Larry Neale)," in *Coagulations: New and Selected Poems* (London: Pluto, 1985), 72–783.

20 I am thinking of the doxa of contemporary affect theory, which often presents itself as if it were the recovery of feeling in critical writing and not — what Cortez would have recognized it as — the endorsement of a deficit. See Lauren Berlant, *Cruel Optimism* (Durham: Duke University Press, 2011): "I believe that its ["weak theory's"] return is in the hope that changing the white noise of politics into something focused but polymorphous can magnetize people to a project of inducing images of the good life that emerge from the sense of loose solidarity in the political that now occupies the ordinary amid the exhausting pragmatics of the everyday" (262). This means finding "loose solidarity" (?) in work that adopts a "politically depressed position, but without seeking repair in an idiom recognizable in the dominant terms" (249).

Compare Cortez: "And like I said, the poems I wrote before going [to Mississippi to participate in the Civil Rights Movement] were concerned with being sad. In Mississippi I learned that you could get rid of a lot of sad feelings, and you didn't have to be isolated, lonely, and frustrated and sitting around without the necessities of life. Because you could do something about it." "Supersurrealist Vision: Interview with Jayne Cortez," in *Heroism in the New Black Poetry: Introductions and Interviews*, ed. D.H. Melham (Lexington: University of Kentucky Press, 1990), 200–201. I think

feels what it knows, and the continuity of the two states is essential to its sense of what radical politics is, of its voluntarism that begins in the chest and then crawls out along the nerves. Atmosphere appears in it as a byproduct of action; not as its subtle and/or titillating substitute. It does not manipulate sadness ("This piece is passing up the motif of sorrow / let it pass"). It presents itself as a challenge. How full, or how empty, can you be? How far can you free yourself of the embarrassment of its inhabitation, and how much of your own vital juices can you transfer into it? The lines represent a position for which even the smallest space that is capable of being filled is more valuable than the largest space that is empty by design, and they are opposed for this reason to a dominant art in which the smallest space that is capable of being emptied (the street, the park) is more valuable than the largest that is capable of being occupied, filled up, lived in, or contested. In addition to this, it recognizes a secret of our own culture. Feeling is not located way out ahead of thinking — thinking doesn't need to "catch up" with our ephemeral sensations of numbness or boredom. This is a class prejudice disguised as a diagnosis of the era. In fact, feeling trails miserably behind thought. Cortez's poetry recognizes that our ideas do not generally arouse in us the feelings that ought to correspond to them, and that can correspond to them if we are willing to do the necessary work, and are fortunate enough to be in a position to do it collectively, as in my own life I have again been recently reminded.

The filling up that has become more centrally significant for Sutherland's recent poetry is of a different kind, but it shares some of the same motivating skepticism related to the construction and dissolution of symbols of emptiness. And the contrast between this skepticism and his attraction to, or dalliance with, psychoanalytic-evolutionary thinking thrashes its way through his recent poetry, from *Jenkins, Moore and Bird* (2013)[21] to the

---

that what Berlant is describing is exactly an "idiom recognizable in the dominant terms." No one else has captured it more succinctly.

21 Sutherland, *Poetical Works,* 371–82.

long poem that follows it, "Sinking Feeling" (2016), in which the contradictory principles of immersion ("nerves and confusion") and development are unhappily unified in the topical metaphor of drowning:

> Then to move it through a doorway blocked up with evacuated footholds laid flat for sliding under you get in. Then at either side the walls too indistinct to mean anything to be symbolic enough except through being made to keep their distance, which is ours too, or to have any role in what is the meaning of their dissipation except by later being cast as its periphery, drowned out in the surging, irritation, bodies in the way, transparency and representations of transparency, reticence and gravity as though in their reality there were no other movement, or any body left, or only one.[22]

Much of "Sinking Feeling" is about violations of the exclusion principle, in its various forms. The poem deals with *ultrafullness,* the presence of two or more distinct objects in the same space, like "a flight deck or the top of a tall building"; or a space that is close and distant simultaneously, "where nothing could be closed, and yet where nothing was without an end or unbound either"; or with moments that represent beginnings and ends at the same time; or that are at once perfectly literal and completely symbolic. The exhaustiveness of its elaborations is likewise both figurative and literal. The language is wearisome to read. It is wearisome to hear, too. In performance Sutherland overstresses its literal exhaustiveness by sounding out all of the metrical passages as if he were shaking his ball and chain. Nothing is left alone to be what it is: and it doesn't matter whether what this is is the totality of objects or nothing at all. The effect extends from the spiritual autobiography that is also the actual mass movement of millions of people to the head that is both losing its hair and already totally bald to the experience of being

---

22 Keston Sutherland, "Sinking Feeling," in *Whither Russia* (Brighton: Barque Press, 2017), n.p.

crowded in by signification and also just being fucking crowded. A roar of competing signification rises up in the poem until only the simplest and most unambiguous language has any hope of being really heard. And it is a part of the work's consummate character (including its consummation of the sequence of poems into which it is inserted) that it is also by turns painfully and infuriatingly aware of this. It offers an overcomplicated account of it: "We wanted to be so simple that even people who could watch the 2015 GOP debates at the Coors Event Center in Colorado could understand us without slitting each other's jugular veins and carotid arteries with sponges full of caramelized phlegm like the butchers of Deir al-Zour." The statement starts out by being just about that simple, and then gets overwhelmed again: the modus operandi is everywhere to be everything in contravention of what is possible: "nothing […] most things […] just a few things […] one particular thing": complex and simple, full up and empty, on fire and extinguished, brilliant and pitch black, submerged and washed up, revived and dead, etc., and therefore *doubly* full, full beyond the capacity of logic to govern what the word means. This applies also to the poem's treatment of symbols. The duplication and splitting of all objects that begins with the ocean itself lies "beyond even the limit case of the pathetic fallacy" because, according to the poet, its symbolism fades into complete literality. It is "transparent" symbolism, the same as what it symbolizes:

> our present reality […] where […] I am now drowning […] where the limits […] seemed inescapably symbolic […] inescapably transparent […] beyond even a limit case of the pathetic fallacy, such as a cloud in the shape of Farmakonisi

My extreme reduction here of a sentence that otherwise is deliberately, unreadably long (full) reduces it to a single point: that the "limits" (the beginning and end) of the poem are "symbols" representing things other than themselves — e.g., the beginning and end of a life — but that the symbols are themselves "transparent." The poem then explains what this means. A cloud in the shape of Farmakonisi would not be a "symbol" of the Greek island of that name because it would simply resemble what it represented in all points of detail. By the same logic, since the beginning of this poem is "transparently" a description of the beginning of a life, it cannot also be held to "symbolize" it. This filling of symbols with literality and vice versa changes the relationship of the author to the "symbols" that he uses. Sutherland doesn't need to attack the symbols into which reality is converted, their congealed immediacy, as he did so vividly in his early poetry, because reality and symbolism loop into one another in a single plane or geometrical space of language pushed to the point of complete immersiveness. Of course, congealed or false immediacies — the symbols that his writing earlier made use of and fought to dissolve — still exist in this poem. Sutherland even says that it doesn't "hurt to call [them] meaning"; and since "meaning" is counterposed in the poem to the "kiss of life," and since throughout this poem all things loop into their opposite in a single space of language pushed to the point of complete immersiveness, so that "meaning" must be death; since "meaning" must be death, the dissolution of symbols, or congealed immediacy, is still something that it could be argued that the poetry wishes to accomplish. But the fullness of this language means that it also comes increasingly to feel less like an attack on the congelation of immediacy than congelation of a different kind, actively the production of a type of viscosity of cognition that retards movement, to the point at which all sense of progress, of acceleration or linear development — of beginnings, middles, and ends, or of anything resembling a "breakthrough" — ceases to apply. And this is how the first section of the poem ends: with the doubling of "fullness" to mean both the exhaustiveness of all objects that are and are not themselves and the experiential viscosity of a language within which it has become impossible to feel oneself accelerating into any kind of freefall:

> Not the way you move, but in, where, past desire, that, before the painless, adjacent extinction, first lasts forever, some-

where is there, who, for now, stranded in your touch, in flight across its furthest stretch, to here, cups its hand to intimate, bids its ruffling gales subside, too far in to surge wide of, as, but I am just thinking, headlong into the lake, storming out, for what, without a head, exhaled at will, sunk in sexual aqueous film, blows out the interiorities, the lot, the orange on the fire stairs, the idiopathic, existing to wish to be picked, persevere, to be shined, when, for the hundredth time cut loose, once they reappear, everyone, being almost there, so that, in sound, not less immaterial than rafts of polystyrene or Rohingya rehydrated into stateless entities, because of the multitude of spermatic reasons, right this way, anxious to tear reality the fuck out, in case its top blisters and is peeled, climaxing, falling off, being repossessed, up to the elbow, where, laced with you, quarterly projections, attachable into the notches' rear fins, worried that my heart would explode, a point is traced, do not go for this you lip-read stitched into the air you wish to empty but will take for now obstructed as it is [...]

"Not the way you move, but in." The phrase seems at first to suggest that it is the "way" that is being negated. A possible continuation of the sentence in line with this expectation would be "Not the way you move, but the *speed* with which you move." Instead, the "Not" obliterates the whole phrase that follows it: instead of "the way you move," this single, enigmatic preposition: "in." Not movement at all, in fact, but the experience of being immersed in an underwater environment in which ideas dissolve and symbols rise up in their place, and that, following the double- or ultra-fullness that was the principle of the poem's first part, is both a general fact about our technically mediated linguistic situation — an abstract geometrical space into which anything can be introduced — and, impossibly, also, the specific sea in which, at the time at which I write, it is possible to say that two hundred people drowned on Tuesday and Wednesday of last week. And it is at this point that something like the grammar of the earlier poetry, of "Mincemeat Seesaw," returns, its interruptions now slowed down, becoming almost aphasic, the movements of a mind scuttling at the bottom of language, watching conjunctions bob and drift above its head. Each forward motion covering the smallest possible distance, like in a legal asylum application process overseen by the British state. The commas create an ambiguity between parataxis and hypotaxis that means that the smallest statements ("but in," "that," "where," "who") can either be read as the beginnings or ends of phrases, as adverbs and pronouns pending clarifications or as questions interjected in a sudden access of frustration, a snapped demand, the need for crude clarity addressed to the system that thrives on sophisticated obscurity: tell me *what* is happening, tell me *where* you mean, tell me what you mean by *that,* by *this,* by *who,* by *you,* tell me how to stop this process that makes the simplest need in my life seem so unfathomably complicated that I want to rip myself to pieces rather than continue with the labor of its fulfilment, and that makes each step forward so insignificant, and that multiplies the number of steps that I have to take to what seems like infinity. Tell me this simply and with human tenderness, give me the opportunity, the power, to say when this will end.

In "Sinking Feeling," Keston Sutherland has written a poem that somewhat resembles, in addition to describing, a waiting room, in which many different kinds of poems and dispositions toward poetry are crammed together side by side, going nowhere, bickering with one another, and from time to time holding one another up. Only Keston could have written something like this. His text puts its reader in the wholly invidious position of an aid worker who is unable to respond to everything and is forced to make difficult choices, even as it splinters into a compendium of different ways of saying we've no choice but to respond with everything we've got. It is contradictory like that. Since once you've spent enough time with it, you begin to notice that amid the crush of different poems and different dispositions towards poetry in "Sinking Feeling," there are also several Keston Sutherlands, also going nowhere, bickering with one another, and from time to time holding one another up. I love that none of them ever stop asking one another "Whose side are you on?"

P.S.

How does all this relate to the desire to reduce the world through the medium of our idea of it? Now, which is to say in March 2020, I still want to learn to reduce the world to what is in front of me. I still want to feel what I know; and I know from my own experience that I cannot feel more than I can say. Keston Sutherland was the first poet to teach me an idiom in which to articulate some of these desires. Before I read his poetry, I barely even knew what a symbol was, and I could not have wished to diminish a world in which all my horizons seemed constantly to be expanding.

And the world is so large and full of possibilities. A building in your neighborhood going up in flames, a letter that you dreaded coming through the letterbox, a government that you hate winning an election, a friend that you loved stepping off a building, etc.

I want to understand possibility in these terms. In a diary of the UK general election of December 2019, a friend wrote of the utterly defeated Labour Party campaign that "[E]nthusiasm is not, in any simple sense, contagious […] it's repellent to see enthusiasm in others when it is not present in yourself."[23] It took me a while to notice the qualification in that statement. "In any simple sense." Why is it then, that enthusiasm should always suggests such a hollow, "simple" kind of possibility? What would enthusiasm look like if it had possibilities of the other kind growing inside of it? Would it look sick? "Contagious"? And who would flinch from it? In the reduced world in which I am currently semi-voluntarily self-isolating, it seems to me that there is no alternative to idealism in class politics, but only various ways of depressing its immune system. We are said con-

---

23 Miri Davidson, "Election Diary," December 2019, in *How To Win*, https://tories-out-propaganda-unit.tumblr.com/.

ventionally to suffer from idealism. Is there also an idealism of the sick?[24]

Those are stupid, overblown questions. I am always so desperate to reach a conclusion. I have wanted so fucking intensely to know what I mean, and the desire has sat in my mouth like a gag:

> over time nothing comes out —
> only the body hardens.
> think of it like you're dragging a tin can
> over to a friend's place, out onto the square, dragging it, like someone else
> soft militant talking too much
> fuck knows what[25]

And will you look at that dash. To be alive now, to be sick and stupid now, to be dragging a tin can now through the square of our ideas and the banal lobbies of our healthy, well-fed idealism, to listen to the rattle it makes — is this one way of producing an idiom? A conclusion. Good singers only need two or three voices. Happiness is knowing our limits. Poetry is the ability not to give a fuck about our end —

---

24 "Words! be sick as I am sick!" That's a line of Frank O'Hara's, though I only know it through Keston Sutherland. Frank O'Hara, "Mayakovsky," *The Collected Poems of Frank O'Hara,* ed. Donald Allen (Berkeley: University of California Press, 1995), 201.
25 Galina Rymbu, "Language Wrecker," trans. Joan Brooks, *Two Lines* 27 (Fall 2017), *Center for the Art of Translation,* https://www.catranslation.org/online-exclusive/language-wrecker/.

8

Mood Music for Wound Building (Some Working Notes on Immediacy)

1

1.1 The desire for immediacy in language is ubiquitous in contemporary art and unites its most radical and its most conservative practitioners.

1.2 We feel our ideas and expressions are *universally* immediate when they can make an instantaneous impression on the widest possible audience. *Particular* immediacies are universal immediacy's raw material; they produce the same effect for audiences of a more restricted size. Ever since large capital came to involve itself in the organization of cultural expression, the abolition or temporary suspension of this distinction between universal and particular immediacy has been a criterion of all genuinely successful political art, and its obfuscation has been a criterion of all reactionary cultural management.

1.3 For capitalist cultural managers, the main instrument for obfuscating the distinction between universal and particular immediacy is the phraseology of authenticity. Authenticity is the medium in which all immediacies seem totally alike.

1.4 In reality, universally available immediacy effects imply a definite level of technical accomplishment. As the amount of capital invested in the production of culture increases, the entry cost of universal immediacy rises also. The proposition remains true notwithstanding the increasingly widespread availability of advanced reproduction technologies said to democratize artistic production.

1.5 Art that is content to base itself on a realistic assessment of what is possible given the existing entry costs to universal immediacy is failed art, and an institutional definition of artmaking that encourages such an assessment is conformist not by accident but by design. But this does not alter the objectivity of the given technical level one single bit.

2

2.1 Radical political art begins with particular immediacy and tries to fight its way to universal immediacy in spite of all the objective barriers that have been set up to prevent this movement. Conservative art (including almost everything that is called contemporary art) begins with universal immediacy and fortifies it with the sandbags of theoretical essentialism.

2.2 Purgative attacks on ideas, speech-forms, or idioms that fall disappointingly short of universal immediacy constitute the method through which conservative art engages in what it calls world-building. Annulment of particular human capacities is what it finds atmospheric. Self-imposition of expressive poverty is what it calls class solidarity.

2.3 The fundamental irony of this position is the way that it responds to experiences of obsolescence. Conservative artists react to their loss of control over the most advanced resources of cultural expression by romanticizing expressive impoverishment. Expressive immediacy is lost to a capital-intensive music and image culture in which all successful works are the result of a complex division of labor. A surrogate immediacy is regained by recourse to an image of social reality that has been purged of all particular idiomatic and communicative force. The response could hardly be more misdirected. It is, just as much as popular hatred for migrants or the unemployed, a testament to the success of the ruling class in making itself seem to disappear.

2.4 The aesthetic value-criterion of difficulty first entered the language during a period in which alterations in the technical reproducibility of art were bringing about enormous transformations in the production of its fundamental aesthetic effects. In the course of this transformation, universal immediacy ceased to fall within the reach of individual bourgeois producers.

2.5 In this sense what art history calls Modernism was always a boring rationalization of powerlessness and an obfuscation of the processes that brought it into being.

2.6 Producers of political art now find themselves in a situation radically unlike the one that was confronted by their counterparts a century previously. The historical association of radical culture with alienation effects or estrangement dates to a period in which radical artists were also still to some degree in control of *immediacy* effects. Now that this is no longer the case, the idea of desiring alienation seems clearly counterintuitive. Desire for immediacy is incomparably more widespread and produces a much wider variety of delusions, misprisions, and political errors, as well as, occasionally, works of beautiful and persuasive clarity.

3

3.1 The commonest of these delusions has to do with a kind of surrogate immediacy. At its most naked, surrogate immediacy is only middle-class alienation made to seem evocatively atmospheric and immersive.

3.2 The surrogate immediacy of middle-class art develops in several stages: (a) first, the loss of attack of institutionalized categories of political analysis is identified and induces a state of alienation from those categories. This alienation continues until (b) the categories begin to be hated. (c) This hatred is resolved by means of fantasized attacks on all forms of particular immediacy, which is to say on our immediate speech-forms, expressive habits, modes of life, and ideas. One conventional way in which these attacks express themselves is in the conjuration of vacant or abandoned space (see: "half-deserted streets"). In a final move, (d) the space thus produced is patronizingly identified with the thoughtless simplicity of working-class reality, whose actual reality has in fact been violently dissolved.

3.3 The result of this sequence is as follows: Alienation is processed into a surrogate immediacy whose appearance is a kind of romanticism of expressive poverty and whose essence is middle-class self-hatred projected into class disdain. Advances in home computing mean that all of this can now be carried out from the comfort of your living room.

3.4 The final social triumph of aesthetic immediacy over aesthetic alienation occurs when even the deepest disillusion with the particular expressive beauty of popular idioms can only be developed in the form of a surrogate immediacy in which skepticism is allegorized as evocative vacancy.

3.5 It is not a contradiction, but an expression of the irrationality of capitalist culture, that the most universal immediacy has its origins in a disguised alienation that itself emerges not out of this or that particular immediacy, but from the mania of middle-class artists to eliminate, purge, and repress it. The class origins of this form of immediacy are not altered when its performers are exemplarily working class.

4

4.1 In the mid-twentieth century, middle-class aesthetics was most commonly justified in metaphysical or existentialist terms. Today, when the degradation of white-collar employment is a preoccupation of the bourgeois mainstream, it is more often justified by the impression of compulsion.

4.2 In a social world in which almost all individuals feel that they need to compete against one another in order to succeed, the ability to give off an aesthetic impression of compulsion begins to rise in value.

4.3 Compulsion effects occur in middle-class art, but they originate in everyday working-class experience. The intrusion of the state into working-class life makes the satisfaction of even ordinary, daily needs seem irresistibly complex and engulfing, as anyone who has undergone, or who has struggled alongside someone going through, a benefits claim or an eviction proceeding will know. Pain de-particularized as an atmospheric property of an aesthetic world takes its license from this basic social experience of everyday struggle that has become unendingly complex and immersive. It mimics an immediacy that has been made to feel overwhelming.

4.4 Compulsion effects make surrogate immediacies seem necessary. They intimate the reasonableness of human displacement and nullification.

4.5 Compulsion effects are in the air. They are aesthetic features of surrogate immediacies and not explicit claims about what it is or is not possible to do. (A minutely descriptive reproduction of what it's like to go through a claim for disability benefits communicates the experience of *compulsion*. The presentation of an empty environment that has been deliberately botched or made to look crude or indistinct constitutes a compulsion *effect*.)

4.6 Compulsion effects are a kind of aesthetic nationalism without the disgusting inconvenience of nations. By making woundedness atmospheric, they aesthetically mimic the ideology of national collective trauma in which real social divisions are usefully submerged.

4.7 Theorists who talk about new aesthetic trends in terms of poor images have taken compulsion effects too seriously. There is no such thing as a poor image. There are images by rich artists trying to conceal their wealth, and there are images by poor ones trying to become individually or collectively wealthy. The transferal of epithets of social class to forms of representation is always a sign that we are dealing with surrogate immediacy and the various effects that obfuscate its real basis in class bias and social resentment. Good artists need to be able to express that knowledge in their art.

4.8 Compulsion effects update working-class solidarity of the Orwellian, upper-class variety for the era of digital communication. Their authors are down and out on the internet. Solidarity of this kind is always a species of ostentatious self-harm.

4.9 Where in fin-de-siècle decadence, rejection of social responsibility took place in the name of sensuous enjoyment, in the twenty-first-century mimicry of sensual displeasure takes place in the name of irresponsibility.

4.10 In an artificial world that has been artfully reduced to its bare minimum of detail, that appears faded or unreal, or that barely coheres in a jumble of grids and geometrical projections, middle-class artists come to feel at last as if they have entered into a structure of more or less total permissiveness. Immersion in this world that has been artfully disfigured or etiolated comes to signal freedom from the obligations of self-care and mutual solidarity. By this means it provides an intense sensation of individual satisfaction in a cultivated atmosphere of general woundedness.

4.11 At the point at which immersion in this world verges on the total, aestheticized self-harm becomes the dominant form of hedonism.

5

5.1 Overwhelming immediacy, surrogate immediacy, particular immediacy, etc., are modes. A realist art today needs to be able to teach itself to switch between them.

5.2 Switching of this type is our *Verfremdungseffekt*. It differs from the alienation effects of the greatest radical art of the twentieth century, because even in its withdrawal from any particular immediacy, and therefore in its contradiction of the implicit claim made by that form of immediacy to constitute a coherent world, it continues to be defined by the immediate sensation of movement.

5.3 In this sense, radical art acknowledges the relative primacy of overwhelming immediacy. There is no particular immediacy that is not a suitable raw material for radical art, but for the great majority of working-class individuals whose immediate circumstances are made by the state to seem overwhelming, the immediate rush of self-determined movement is too vital to be dispensed with.

6

6.1 Currently universal immediacy has many of the characteristics of a surrogate immediacy. Vast quantities of human labor are expended on the accomplishment of this outcome. No trick is spared in finding new ways to make non-specific pain and implied emptiness seem contemporary, sublime, and overwhelming.

6.2 To talk about the entire division of labor, structure of ownership, ensemble of technical resources and recording media, machinery of distribution, and raw giftedness involved in the making of mass art in terms of universal immediacy is an egregious simplification undertaken in the name of immediacy itself.

6.3 A materialist expressionism today must find a way to make use of the crude assertion that while bourgeois art makes immediacy seem as if it were structural, a radical art has to make structure feel immediate.

9

"Language Is for Fucking Idiots": On Porpentine Charity Heartscape

Dear Florence,

It is 1:30 on Saturday afternoon, January 12, 2019. You have asked me to write something about poetry and anti-fascism. I am trying to work out where to start.

I've wanted to try to write down my thoughts about this since at least February 2017, when I was drawn into the campaign to close down the neo-reactionary art gallery in Hackney that had started running talking shops for fascists. It feels surprising to me that that was two years ago already, that it's election year in the US next year. 2020 felt like an age away then. That moment around Trump's election felt so chaotic to me; it was like a hole had been punched into my expectations and suddenly all of these things of which I had been dimly aware were slithering around inside of them with horrible unignorable clarity. I was so frightened by everything that was going on around us. It seems important to me now to be able to admit that we were not thinking very clearly, to be candid about it.

And now that I have the space to get my thoughts down about all of that stuff its significance seems to have diminished again: the lights have come back up, the monsters in the closet testify that they were only doing business, the libertarian financiers creep back into the shadows, and Trump stands alone in the White House, lost in thought, his Nuremburg Rally a table of hamburgers.

I don't mean that we can breathe a deep sigh of relief. Obviously that would be fucking unconscionable. But I do think that to start making work that was obsessed exclusively with an imminent fascist state-takeover would be a political and aesthetic error. Massive racist "movements" are a part of Western liberal societies today, not opposed to them. Cultural impulses that expressed themselves in opposition to the state were injected into the bloodstream of liberal commodity culture decades ago, as action films and structural adjustment programs and daytime TV, and as the War on Drugs and Terror and Welfare Cheats and Economic Migrants and then as revenge pornography and Twitter mobs and shooter survival and little Maddie and all of the other corporate-sponsored hypertensives that have been working their way through the body politic for years, to give Rupert Murdoch his long drawn-out symbolic erection. This stuff just didn't exist in the same way a century ago. What does it mean to want to politicize aesthetics in circumstances like ours? Surely the answer can't be the same as it was in 1936. It can't be "Brecht."

This just as a brief attempt to set out where I'm coming from. I should also add, since a lot of what I'm going to argue might seem to be dismissive of the idea of an anti-fascist art as such, that I don't think that the rejection of an explicitly anti-fascist poetry means that there's no need for anti-fascist politics. I am just saying that the way in which fascism is configured today means that the culture of fascism is not made predominantly by fascists. The obvious corollary of that statement is that a powerful anti-fascist art won't have much to say about fascist ideology either.

So that will do by way of introduction.

¯_(ツ)_/¯

All of this stuff has become tied up recently in my head with the famous Walter Benjamin quotation about fascism aestheticizing politics.[1] I had thought that I understood what Benjamin meant by that statement without needing to re-read what he wrote. I had begun to use it as a kind of shorthand for something that it seemed to me to be important to describe. But then I went back to his essay and realized that he was talking about something else, and now I feel like my misunderstanding has to do at least in part with the way in which fascist culture has changed in the period since his death. I'll try to explain the misunderstanding as clearly as I can.

This is a straightforward way of presenting it: the impulse to make politics beautiful is distinct from the belief that beauty is a property of political ideas. Benjamin was writing about fascism as a tendency that would beautify politics by conflating it with heroic, technically advanced warfare. His intention was to revise a Marxist argument: fascism was a way for the masses to make use of the most advanced potential of the existing forces of production (or destruction) "while preserving traditional property relations."[2] By contrast, in my own mind Benjamin's phrase had

---

[1] "Its [Fascism's] self-alienation has reached the point where it can experience its own annihilation as a supreme aesthetic pleasure. Such is the aestheticizing of politics, as practiced by fascism. Communism replies by politicizing art"; Walter Benjamin, "The Work of Art in the Age of Its Mechanical Reproduction," in *The Work of Art in the Age of Its Technological Reproducibility: And Other Writings on Media,* eds. Michael W. Jennings, Brigid Doherty, and Thomas Y. Levine (Cambridge: Harvard, 2008), 42.

[2] "In technological terms it can be formulated as follows: only war makes it possible to mobilize all of today's technological resources while maintaining property relations": "The Work of Art," 41. This was exactly what Marx in his famous Preface to *A Contribution to the Critique of Political Economy* had claimed to be impossible. Benjamin's revision of Marx's argument about the contradiction between the "forces" and "relations" of production (which is to say, between the technical potential of society and the ability of capitalism to realize it), suggests that the contradiction can be removed within capitalism (a possibility that Marx had denied) by the channelling of those technical means towards destructive ends. Technical potential is therefore realized through a kind of sadism. I'll say more about this later on. Karl Marx, *A Contribution to the Critique of Political Economy,* trans. N.I. Stone (Chicago: Charles H. Kerr, 1904).

come to refer to people for whom violent ideas were beautiful, who took pleasure in the solecisms and crudeness and brutality of racist, authoritarian political speech, and who experienced in all of those properties a kind of counterfeit aesthetic enjoyment. The first case of the "aestheticization of politics" applies most straightforwardly to people who experience their lives with the greatest fullness and intensity in situations of violent militarized conflict, the second to people who experience them with the greatest fullness and intensity on Twitter. The account of fascist aesthetics in "The Work of Art in the Age of Mechanical Reproduction" continues to be relevant to the political proceedings of certain balkanized strips of Northern Syria and to the suburbs of outer Moscow, but the account that I had wrongly attributed to it provides a better description of the relationship between art and politics for the homeowners of Swindon and Worthington, Ohio.

I might seem to be tying myself up in a contradiction. On the one hand I am arguing that a fascistic culture reproduces itself without the intercession of actual fascists. On the other hand I am describing a kind of metamorphosis in the aestheticization of politics that Benjamin said was fascism's defining cultural characteristic. Which is it? Does fascism disappear into the structure of consumer personhood under the liberal capitalist state, or does it revive itself in the face of a violent capitalist culture, as the aestheticization of aggressive political language?

For me, the point of overlap between a fascistic culture within liberal capitalism and explicit fascist conviction is the increasing technical potential to use language as a means to satisfy violent urges. To the extent that the desire for violent collective purification can be satisfied within the domain of individual consumption under the stewardship of the constitutional state, the appeal of outright fascism will tend to decline. To the extent that the beauty of this violence is experienced *in language,* its appeal will tend to increase. The same technical advances that incorporate into liberal capitalism those tendencies to aestheticized violence that were originally the distinguishing cultural characteristic of fascism, drive people to make their own sadistic pleasure in language and at the same time vastly increase their ability to use it in order to inflict harm on total strangers. Fascist ideology, shorn of its militarist culture, then becomes a culture unto itself: fascist language is the preeminent form of violent language, even if fascist art, fascist militias, and fascist state theory have all long since been superseded. Fascism is in this sense neither the inevitable outcome of capitalist development, nor something that it can mechanically overcome, but instead a dialectical operation of historically constituted techniques on socially constituted urges.

For the rest of this essay, I'll try to say a little more about a body of work whose anti-fascism can be understood in these terms.

¯_(ツ)_/¯

Here is a comment on the aestheticization of politics circa June 2018:

> The promise of the internet and neoliberalism is that everyone gets to be a cop. Everyone gets to be the drone pilot of *something*. You can't control your life and you're trapped in an infinite self-replicating hellscape of concrete with no kinship and no culture and the sky is on fire and the sea is choking on plastic and everything's shit but by god you can team up on some poor homeless bitch who no one will miss and gangbang that butterfly on a wheel. You can molest the girl with a dick at your university, you can forcefeed your autistic kid bleach, you can do anything but change a thing that matters.[3]

---

3 Porpentine Charity Heartscape, *the shape you make when you want your bones to be closest to the surface, Slime Daughter*, 2018, http://www.slimedaughter.com/games/twine/closest; emphasis original. Available along with all of Porpentine's other games at www.slimedaughter.com/games. A smart summary that makes lots of useful points is Siri Lee, "Game Review: the shape you make when you want your bones to be closest to the

This is a passage concerned with some of our own technological possibilities. In some respects its line of argument seems quite similar to Benjamin's. For Benjamin's "[Fascism] sees its salvation in granting expression to the masses — but on no account granting them rights," read "Everyone gets to be the drone pilot of something." In both cases the language describes the aesthetics of violent acting out. Whereas for Benjamin the price of identification with the superhuman is passionate absorption in the fantasy of bodily annihilation, for the author of the passage quoted above, the price of individual emancipation is collusion in the bodily degradation of feminized others. In both cases aesthetics amounts to a sensation of activity that doesn't "change a thing that matters," with the further qualification that the sensation feels best when it is expressed either as liquidation of the feeble human body or as aggressive domination of a wounded, exposed, disgusting, or defenseless third party. This is the ecstatic fascist intersection of torture and what now goes by the name of self-care, the kind of beaming, sado-positive therapy for which a figure like Milo Yiannopoulos was briefly famous. It is beautiful insofar as we are the person it is for.[4] The main difference between the passage I have just quoted and the Benjamin text is, of course, that the former nowhere uses the word "fascism." It says "the internet and neoliberalism," but it could just as well say "the dominant society," or "social networks," or "today."

---

surface," *Critical Videogames Studies,* October 16, 2018, updated October 17, 2018, https://uofcmediastudies.wixsite.com/vgs2018/blog/game-review-the-shape-you-make-when-you-want-your-bones-to-be-closest-to-the-surface.

4   When I Google "gangbang that butterfly on a wheel," the first thing that comes up is some porn film on Pornhub. When I Google "butterfly on a wheel," I get a high-concept 2007 thriller starring Pierce Brosnan, about a man who concocts a fake abduction scenario in order to mentally torture the guy who has been having an affair with his wife. Later I get to Alexander Pope's "Epistle to Arbuthnot," our final destination, a passage in which the poet vindicates his own practice of writing brilliant, elaborate satires against pathetic, low, and undeserving targets. It is funny that this most elegant metaphor for punching down should have originated in the work of the person who was most exquisitely accomplished in the art of doing exactly that.

It is not arguing that "the internet and neoliberalism" are fascist, but that those characteristics that almost a century ago would have been associated with fascist art are today widespread aspects of everyday culture. Could anyone today possibly deny this? For Marinetti, and for the Fascists of the 1910s more generally, war was beautiful "because it enriches a flowering meadow with the fiery orchids of machine-guns." It was beautiful because it mixes "gunfire, barrages, cease-fires, scents, and the fragrance of putrefaction."[5] For the Reddit Marinettis of 2016, the internet was beautiful because it mixed rhetorical cock-waving with the literal image of domination in fucking, and the conspiratorial satisfactions of a fantasized whole with the abrupt emptiness of a loading screen. In circumstances like these, Max Horkheimer's famous remark about fascism and capitalism has become a truism for the theoretical edification of prudes: the person who should remain silent about fascism is not the one who is unwilling to talk about capitalism, not primarily the Madeleine Albrights and Timothy Snyders of this world, but the person who fails to talk openly about ego-collapse, sexual violence, or themselves. Everyone knows that capitalism invests heavily in all three.

¯_(ツ)_/¯

The last block quotation is drawn from a text-based computer game by the game designer Porpentine Charity Heartscape, *the shape you make when you want your bones to be closest to the surface*. It was commissioned by the Museum of Contemporary Art Chicago and released sometime in mid-2018. It is impossible to say how far into the game the quote comes, because the work itself is built out of a congeries of hypertext links that constantly loop back on themselves and deposit the player at an earlier stage of its narrative movement. Like many of Porpentine's text-games, *the shape you make* is preoccupied with

---

5   This and the previous quotation cited in Benjamin, "The Work of Art in the Age of Its Mechanical Reproduction," 41.

world creation, the obliquities of self-narration in fidelity to the trauma that prohibits it, and generic cultural form, the satirical manipulation of which this author has mastered like perhaps no other writer working today. Her games are a new kind of psychic pointillism, a constantly decomposing mental breakdown in text-format, dispersed like solar dust into the pixelated debris. I know of no one who has done more in obsessively re-imagining the formal uses of the web browser in levering open the shut-up, wounded, online head.

the shape you make reminds me in certain ways of the trajectory of a discussion on poetry and anti-fascism in which I participated in November 2018.[6] I had wanted to talk, at that event, about the role in our psychic lives of stereotyped images of capital-letter Fascism. My idea was to try to open a discussion about how our wider culture has become saturated with those images, of crude Teutons and equilateral Klanspeople, and I thought I would talk about how this saturation begins, at the first moment that we sit down at our desks in our state-run schools to begin dutifully to internalize our state-sanctioned syllabi. I had it in my head that we would talk about how successful this operation is, since the same process that establishes the icons of racism and authoritarianism as foreign icons and as lessons from the past is also the one that allows us to become convinced of the essential otherness of fascism to our own lives. I wanted to say how in my own work I try to manipulate those symbols like puppets, to stick my hands into them and make their tongues wag in disgusting, lascivious mimicry of the pallid, wagging fingers of their consumer audiences; and I wanted to say that our art could burst from their puppet-torsos like blissful alien jack-in-the-boxes, screaming the news that this was a new genetic

---

6   Some questions I wrote down for the discussion can be accessed at "Questions for an Anti-Fascist Culture (Nov. 2018)," https://bit.ly/2RwDpin. A partial transcript of the conversation is available under the title "Some communal thoughts on poetry and anti-fascist culture," *Poetry Emergency: A North West Radical Poetry Festival*, November 23–24, 2018, https://poetryemergency.files.wordpress.com/2019/05/some-communal-thoughts-on-poetry-and-anti-fascist-culture-1.pdf.

mutation in the "aestheticization of politics" itself: a novel strain of it, metastasizing in the ego-conduct of liberal people who live in liberal capitalist societies in which almost every impulse that was associated with fascists circa 1936 can now be satisfied every evening by even the most upstanding champion of democracy and human rights. (Everyone knows at least two people who prove it.)

What we mostly talked about at the event instead was violence, about violence in left-wing poetry and in fascist culture, and about how to discriminate between the two, and we argued with one another about whether we needed to make art that was less or merely differently violent; and I was too slow-witted at the time to realize that this was in fact the conversation that I had wanted in slightly modified terms, since we were its primary subject.

¯_(ツ)_/¯

But assume that Benjamin is right, and that fascist aesthetics is a kind of travesty of the gap between actual human reality and technically determined human potential. How do we relate ourselves to that potential?

One way would be to try to find some method of saying what it is: to rip out from the thin, insulting air of Google and Twitter some image of the life that they can never depict. And for many years this has been my own answer. I have wanted my poetry to be the immediate realization of existing technical potential. I have given to that potential the name of communism, and I have burned through successive definitions of that term with the enthusiasm of Parisian street demonstrators for luxury cars. I am now faced with the sensation that this has been a fruitless exercise, and a sort of expressive masochism. What other approaches can be conceived of?

Porpentine's games provide another answer to the same problem. They don't try to overcome the gap between human reality and technically determined potential, but to light a fire in it. Unfinished highways of feeling loop through her text segments in almost imperceptible outline, standing out in relief against the desktop-wallpaper greens and oranges of their in-browser backdrops — an affective stage scenery retrenched and then retrenched again to its drowsy, dogmatic degree zero. The non-existent knife that has a central role in the narrative of her 2014 game *With Those We Love Alive* is at once the conscious emblem of this materialism of the unrealized and the virtuosic contraction of its telescopic absences to the dimensions of a simple plot point.[7] Who is still afraid of the dark?

the shape you make provides this spacious quality of Porpentine's work with a few more contour lines. Essential to its overall structure is a kind of complex of incompletions: incompletion of its (apparently) autobiographical narration of early media consumption and of its repressive association with shame; incompletion in the account of the intrusion of those early experiences into later practices of intimate care; and incompletion in the game's biting criticism of internet culture and its barely-speculative future of fully privatized exclusion mechanisms. The prurient desire of the game-player to access more exquisite vignettes of defenseless childhood suffering is anticipated in the game itself: enough click-throughs brings you to a screen that reads

> art is an obsession that buries you inside the beauty until you can't see it anymore, you disappear, sacrificed so others can look at it from the outside and see what you were dreaming when you started.

This is who you are, player: the "other who can look […] from the outside," and see into passages of self-description of an almost unbearably frank and compromised intimacy. It would be very easy for the game, or for the writer of it, having painstakingly established this relation, to feel violated by its asymmetry, and to formulate its (and her) anticipation of the reader's

---

7 Porpentine Charity Heartscape, *With Those We Love Alive*, Slime Daughter, 2014, http://slimedaughter.com/games/twine/wtwla/.

grasping intrusiveness as a kind of revenge — a comeuppance achieved by way of intellectual mastery, through the humiliating demonstration to that person, the reader, now a kind of transfixed analysand, of just who they are, and by shoving down their throat the evidence of their own violent, insatiable greed. "The entire world is connected by an ethereal lifestream of information and the best people can think to do with it is participate in human sacrifice." But that doesn't happen, here, in those words. The tone is instead suggestive, Schumannesque. The beauty. Ghost variations. A few, skeletal notations of heat death. The gameplay is not an intelligence test.

And in this sense, it is the opposite of the most basic metaphor of fascist self-understanding. Fascists imagine themselves in a very particular way. In Klaus Theweleit's famous study of the writings of German Freikorpsmen, *Male Fantasies,* the structure is laid out again and again:

> The fascists were not projecting when they singled out Friedrich Ebert from the Left for a certain grudging admiration. They sensed that this man (whom Erhard Lucas fittingly describes as presenting a "brow of iron" to all demands from the Left) would not allow a single drop of the stream to seep through; he would not rest until he had crushed all attempts to form soviets, to socialize particular areas of production, or to organize a republican army. Ebert's first love was his organization, the Party. The party in power: large, rigid blocks; dams [...][8]

> For the Fuehrer's "wife," in that fascist ritual, was the unconscious of the masses who were pouring into block formations. "And now the screams of 'Heil!' erupt, becoming overwhelming, like some all-fulfilling wave that rips everything along with it. Fifty thousand voices merge into a single cry of 'Heil Hitler!' Fifty thousand arms shoot out in salutes.

---

8 Klaus Theweleit, *Male Fantasies,* Vol. 1 (Minneapolis: University of Minnesota Press, 1987), 384.

Fifty thousand hearts beat for this man who is now striding, bareheaded, through the narrow passage formed by all those thousands."⁹

Theweleit's argument about fascists who imagine themselves as blocks without gaps, penetrable orifices, or vacuums is a part of his explication of the relationship of male fascists to women. His argument that these fascists have yet to be born means to suggest a quite different way of thinking about human ego development than the one with which we are familiar from Freudian psychoanalysis. Instead of undergoing the incorporation of an internal super-ego representing the father as a resolution of the Oedipus complex, the fascist personality is formed through the constant disciplining of the body in the process of the military drill. It emerges through its bending and welding into the continuous, unbroken surface of the collective block person: the nation or military parade.

The threat of personal dissolution outside of this relationship of violent male fraternity is, predictably, warded off through explosions of frantic violence. In the sight of the quivering, lifeless flesh of battlefield enemies, in their blood and shit turned outwards and commingled and externalized, the Freikorps man discharges the anxiety he feels at the prospect of his own dispersal or fragmentation. He blacks out and is reborn. The first screen of *the shape you make*: "One of my first memories is a bowl of blood and flesh in a bedroom."

Fascists imagine themselves as blocks because the idea that their personalities might contain holes or gaps is unbearable to them. They need to be impenetrable, complete, positively constipated with their own heroism. Squadrists, ex-syndicalist theorists of the total state, Nazi stormtroopers, fans of the band Skrewdriver, and racist 4Chan users represent the unity-in-difference of this need not only to be whole, but to be full.[10] How

---

9 Ibid., 435.
10 In Newcastle in 2015 I walked down a hill behind a right-wing biker with a patch on his jacket that said *The UK Is Full*. And he was.

does this relate to the argument I made earlier, about language being the point of contact between a fascistic culture without fascists, on the one hand, and the transformation in the fascist aestheticization of politics, on the other? I said there that insofar as the aestheticization of politics still occurs, it does so in language. I also said that it was here more than anywhere else that fascist cultural tendencies realized themselves in fascist politics, and that it was a real contradiction of capitalist social relationships that the same process that allows capital to interiorize fascism, in the same way that a child might grow up to interiorize her adult persecutors, also produces new, consciously revolutionary fascists through the new technical affordances of language to hurt, brutalize, and cause pain.

But why is this the case? If fascism has been deprived of its mastery over the sadistic aesthetics of existing technical potential (which is to say, over the politics of war), what kind of language allows it to sustain its own ideology?

The usefulness of Theweleit's argument to my mind is this. It allows us to see what fascist language tries to achieve. Fascism becomes conscious and theoretically aware in language because theoretical language is, or feels, block-like and gapless; and because it is block-like and gapless language, more than any other kind, that does duty as a bludgeoning instrument for the infliction of intellectual injury.[11] While in every other domain of social life, advanced capitalist relations have interiorized the sadistic urges that previously sought expression in fascist opposition to the state,[12] in the scene of communication it has given fascist theory an immense new lease on life, as the one solid,

---

11 So, to be specific, my argument is that the gaplessness of a widespread neo-fascist conspiracy theory like the "Eurabia theory," or, still better, the "Cultural Marxist" theory, is attractive to individuals used to attacking other people on the internet not because it explains anything, but because it seems like an effective instrument for meting out punishment. The titles assigned to Youtube clips of television debates featuring fascists and liberals famously bear this out. Fascist theory is attack theory.

12 Which is to say, the new state, the liberal democratic state of constitutional conventions and universal enfranchisement, formed either in belated emulation of the central capitalist powers or as the direct consequence of

impenetrable block that individual men and women are able to call their own. This is the latest stage in the dialectic of fascist culture, its aestheticization of politics distorted into the tendency to find the most bestialized and persecutory speech-habits at once beautiful and sexually arousing.

We are now faced with the task of imagining what these historical transformations mean for anyone whose ambition is not to aestheticize politics, but to politicize aesthetics. Porpentine gets the main problem into focus: "Language is for fucking idiots. [...] I don't really know a lot about abstract concepts. I only know about the stuff I'm interested in or the tiny hyper-specific details that I focus on." Her games are sustained elaborations on that instinct, the formal antithesis to the cutting edge of conceptual language. And that they somehow manage to be this literally and not only in some amiable metaphorical sense is so astonishing to me, and so moving. Again, the first sentence of *the shape you make*: "One of my first memories is a bowl of blood and flesh in a bedroom." Replaced at the second screen with "Me and my siblings weren't born in hospitals." How many cancelled possibilities are strung out across these two screens and twenty-three words? How many times do you have to read the second statement before it emerges for you as a comment on the first, before "hospitals" and "bowl of blood and flesh" assert their elective affinity? How often do you have to be reborn through the game's click-through HTML loops into the scene of the first screen before you realize that this scene of your birth as the game's player is not primarily an enigmatically evocative statement about violence and sexual desire — the stress held on "bedroom" — but a description of a home birth that connotes (at least for anyone unfamiliar with normal homebirths, which is probably the majority of the game's players) stillbirth, or abortion? And what does it mean for clarity to be withheld like this, and why is it that this birth that is also the cancellation of birth, measured out not in abstract space but in the lived time of

---

military defeat by them — since it was in these conditions that interwar fascism emerged and its specific relationship to violence was elaborated.

my own fallible head, in the dimensions of my own distraction and insensitivity, and of my indifference to tiny details — why is it that it cuts so deeply into the heart of the central organizing metaphor both of conscious fascists and of the violent, repetitive video games that have usurped so much of the social libido that they used to be able to monopolize, into the scene of "palingenesis," rebirth or reawakening, where we come to life as gapless blocks, with our health bars replenished, screaming insults at the weak?

Language is for fucking idiots.

The fascist who thinks he is a block, a hard, integral object without gaps, internal fissures, or breaks — this fascist is convenient for us, liberal and radical anti-fascists alike, because he is not like us, because he shares none of our DNA, and because the imperative that he suggests to us is simple, reassuring, and familiar. It is merely the imperative, broadcast to us by our teachers from the earliest days of our infancy, that we ensure a rigorous regime of self-hygiene! And this is a fundamental fact about contemporary capitalist societies. Just as the impulses towards obscene violence, ecstatic domination, spectacularized militarism, and the hysterical persecution of vulnerable, unclean others that were the hallmarks of the fascist movements of the 1930s are now largely internalized to the private domain of the individual liberal consumer, so too has the tendency to aestheticize politics, once the distinguishing tendency of fascist artists, become a leitmotiv of the dominant liberal political theory. As this process gathers pace, mainstream media hysteria about an impending fascist takeover increases necessarily in proportion.

But fascists are not towering granitic blocks with no gaps or breaks. They are tiny nuclei of ideas afloat in great cytoplasmic seas of unconceptualized frustration and directionlessness. The tendency to plump for the former conception instead of the latter is fundamental to the contemporary aestheticization of politics, which is also the reason why any essay on anti-fascism and poetry is also compelled to explain why there is now no such thing as fascist art.

I cut the words "I think" from the preceding paragraph. My life up to now has been a fight for conceptual clarification. I am not used to holding space open. I have not yet learned to use what doesn't exist as a surgical (musical) instrument.

I am not alone in this. Klaus Theweleit's magnificent two-volume book finishes with an abrupt, mirthful ellipsis, as if this might amount to an adequate response to the history of attempts by male artists to overleap the distance between reality and technical potential. His fundamentally non-artistic response to an almost insoluble compositional problem shows how easy it is to fail to take beauty seriously.[13]

One is not born a fascist, one is reborn, palingenetically, at the moment when one's gaps are closed up. This is the infinite possibility of systematic thinking, a compositional procedure as flexible and as miraculously susceptible to permutation as three dots crammed together at the end of a sentence. It is how we respawn again and again into the first screen of our lives, a bowl of blood and flesh in a bedroom, exhilarated in the re-emergence of this stillbirth, shoveling worlds into a system.

Porpentine's games are the closest thing I know to a successful anti-fascist art in the specific sense that I am discussing, because they are among the only works that I can think of that take absolutely seriously the task of composing with what doesn't yet exist. This is not negative capability, apophasis, or the jaded specter of nineteenth-century Romantic irony. It is alien to the clichés of "atmosphere" or "tone," which are anyway hateful non-words that do for aesthetics roughly what "diseased migrant caravan" does for politics. All of the above-mentioned tendencies are perfectly compatible with art made by fascists and would

---

[13] Theweleit is not to blame for this inadequacy. My point is only that his book tries to undermine block-like concepts in what is ultimately a highly conceptual way. The ellipsis stands for the openness that self-assertive advocates of conceptual gaplessness (revolutionary men who brook no dissent) are congenitally afraid of. But it does not compose a space for it. The end…

continue to be prominent features of fascist culture if it were not for the fact that the great majority of the candidate-artists are now in fact smiling, hygienic political liberals with the portfolio webpages to prove it. What makes Porpentine a great artist is not her fragments or uncertainties, mysteries, or doubts, but her singular ability to find ways of holding open with the steadiness of surgical forceps all of the distances that have grown up within and between us and that threaten to collapse again the moment we open our mouths. By making those distances into compositional materials, she opens a way out of the culture of fascism and anti-fascism in which we loop around, as if in a kind of endless, distorting hall of mirrors.

10

Letter to Lotte L.S.:
On Sean Bonney

Dear Lotte,[1]

How are you? Thank you for sending me your pamphlet a couple of months ago. I see that you've made another one since with some of John Barker's writing — I'd like to have that one too, if there are any of those stamps still going. But I wanted to respond first to your poem and its "p.s.," and to say some things about what felt important in it to me, and also to try to get down some of my feelings about Sean Bonney's recent poetry, which appears in the vicinity of yours, as one of its many points of reference.

I want to say first though how grateful I am for the poem and for what it works through and exposes. I know from reading your writing (not just in the pamphlet) how hostile you are to

---

[1] This letter was written in response to an untitled and unpaginated pamphlet distributed by Lotte L.S. in early 2020. In what follows, unattributed quotations in the letter itself or in footnotes are taken from the pamphlet. As a first step, it may also help to set out the contents of the edition notice: "Written in Great Yarmouth June 2019 & Athens December 2019. Printed January 2020. Anti-copyright. Free to distribute, copy, borrow, steal. Images show anti-NATO riots in Iceland in 1949, protests against George H.W. Bush's visit to Iceland in 1983, and nootka lupine in 2019. Any donations to Andrými social centre in Reykjavík."

the idea that any of us should have to expose any of ourselves to a poetry world that is in its own aspirational way just the GCHQ[2] in miniature, and I feel the same way, and always have, that it is a necessity (and also just better for our life, for life) to keep our heads down. That isn't quite the kind of exposure that I mean. One of the things that I think makes your book so unusual is its direct assertion of some actual principles for poetry, from the "Anti-copyright" down to the provisional rules for the first person plural (more on that at the end) which after so much argument and counterargument you finally set out in the postscript. And your book shows that those principles are not just dogmatic inheritances, but that we need to find ways — to work for ways — to expose them in our lives, and to expose our lives to them. So that's closer to what I'm trying to talk about, and this kind of exposure is much more interesting to me than the kind of pseudo-drama of self-revelation that might induce the poetry GCHQ to award one of its £3,000 prizes.

I expect that this will seem more like an essay disguised as a letter than vice versa. I'm struggling to keep things separate at the moment, as in, this is an (inadequate) attempt to say something about your poetry, the way it addresses collectivity, its treatment of loss, memory, fidelity to shared experience, etc. But also I can't keep those things apart in my own head from my own unstable relation to Sean's death and the filter of poetry readings, confusion, numbness, blogposts, diatribes, Crass lyrics, Halloween parties, and mental breakdowns through which I'm only sometimes able to catch sight of it, an *Accattone* in the squat cinema of my mind, showing in incalculable fits and starts. And I first met you at the Poetry and Emergency conference in November 2018, which was also — will now always be — the last time that I saw him, dead drunk and being put into a taxi talking about how he wanted to go to his hotel room to read John

---

[2] GCHQ stands for Government Communications Headquarters. It is the UK equivalent of the NSA and an important part of the global "Five Eyes" digital spying network.

Wieners, like John Wieners was someone who would take care of him, and this is just one stretch of time; but it feels longer in one case than the other.

And essays are usually meant to hold all of that stuff at arm's length, which is why this isn't (why I don't want this to be) an essay, but letters are meant to be answerable, and I'm not sure that this one is. There are too few questions in it, and probably too many presumptions — you can point them out if you have the time for it. I would like to know whether you feel now like you're on the other side of the poem — whether the pledge at the end of your "p.s." continues to feel sustainable. Does it? When I first read the pamphlet it felt to me like a very stable object: its joints and the points of intersection of its materials seemed not only "well judged," but also as if the whole thing might have just fallen into place, like a jigsaw that had done you the favor of self-assembling, and despite how ludicrous and ungenerous that kind of admiration is I carried on feeling it even while I was puzzling my way through the remark towards the end of the postscript, that "[f]or a while" you had "stopped thinking about the poem before going to sleep, stopped reciting it on late night bike rides home, stopped staring at it on a lit screen." Theories are hard to let go of, they survive the greatest amount of contravening evidence — this is one of the tedious lessons that the December general election is now famous for having re-re-taught us — and it was only when I went back to the essays you published last year to find pieces of familiar language from the poem and the postscript staring out at me, in new and different configurations, that I understood how much re-working was at the root of the apparent stability of the book that you assembled and published. So there go those stretches of time again. I'd be really interested to know how they seem to you right now.

> For a long time I have considered the meaning of the point of no return.[3]

---

[3] Quoted in Lotte L.S., "'Not to speak about / only to speak nearby,'" *Poetry Foundation Blog*, May 13, 2019, https://www.poetryfoundation.org/har-

So. It's easy to read the poem as a single elegy, with Rojava as its main elsewhere and Haukur as its main subject. That particular, excruciating fact of distance in it: how can we relate to a revolutionary armed struggle, when what we live in is an ongoing, occurring circus of reactionary consent? How can we represent the decisions of those who have died in it, when we are where we are?

I had been thinking about that question throughout January. A quotation from Fassbinder that had been doing the rounds on the internet got stuck in my head:

> People haven't learned how to love. The prerequisite for loving, without dominating the other, is your body learning, from the moment it leaves the womb, that it can die. When you accept that a part of life is death, you have no more fear of it and you don't fear any other "conclusions." But as long as you live in terror of death, you react likewise to the end of a relationship, and as a result, you pervert the love that does exist.[4]

There's a sense of cliché in all of this. Death as a part of life: a bohemian's exercise in titillating the sub-editors. But I had begun to feel fear of death (not only of my own) perverting my thinking about politics too, and I wanted to challenge that habit, to think openly about some of the possibilities that I had shut myself up against. I felt that I had become too preoccupied with the point of no return to the exclusion of everything that we can presume to lie beyond it, and also that, in equating that point with death, I had forgotten that part of what lies beyond it is

---

riet/2019/05/not-to-speak-about-only-to-speak-nearby. Now expanded in *A town, three cities, a fig, a riot, two blue hyacinths, three beginnings, five letters, a "death", two solitudes, façades, four loose dogs, a doppelgänger, a likeness, three airport floors, thirty-six weeks...*, Tripwire Pamphlet Series #10, https://tripwirejournal.com/tripwire-pamphlet-series/.

4 Norbert Sparrow and Rainer Werner Fassbinder, "'I Let the Audience Feel and Think': An Interview with Rainer Werner Fassbinder," *Cinéaste* 8, no. 2 (1977): 21.

a number of different forms of survival, some of which might prove less cramped and less fearful than the imperative to survive per se. On top of that I was feeling happier than I had, and wanted to take some pleasure in fucking things up again. We pervert the love that does not exist, also.

Yesterday, cycling towards Bloomsbury from Hackney, from the street market where much of my current life plays out to a place where many of my earliest political experiences took place, I tried to figure some of this out. I thought about the film about Anna Campbell's life that the BBC broadcast a year or so ago. Perhaps you remember it? There's a moment in that documentary where Jamie Janson talks about why he went to fight in Rojava. He says (as I remember) something striking about why he needed to leave his life and go there — that he had come to feel that compared to his own political activity the Kurdish struggle represented the "real" revolution, and that was why he needed to be a part of it. There is something consciously, devastatingly naïve in the simplicity of that idea, and at the same time we all know exactly what he means. A "real revolution" is *not-this,* it isn't NGO work or opinion ed. hand-wringing or academic radicalism. It's the situation in which our desire for a transformed social life is externalized, is no longer just a smear of impulses playing out inside our own heads, like a bloody mess, an abstract painting, a gibberish of nineteenth-century words, idea salads for salaried intellectuals that real people just aren't going to have the time for, is ACTUAL REAL LIFE, "real" to the point that people are willing to give up their lives for it. "In the English-speaking world, where none of us know anything except how to kill," that kind of idealism is systematically killed off (is "tragic," "poignant," etc.), which is why among other reasons it sucks so much to touch back down in its principles of objectivity in Luton.[5]

I found myself thinking about how your poem deals with that commitment to the point of no return in its aftermath. Revolu-

---

[5] "preparing for the plane, Luton, rain, / England / its principles of objectivity[.]"

tionary politics MUST be made real and conclusive even at the most extreme cost of one's own life; the pledging or staking of life is essential to the reality of the transformation that it brings about and acts unerringly as the proof of it. At the same time, death in armed struggle is brutal, unheroic, inconclusive, and uneventful. It leaves us to live with the unanswerable; it is inflicted from the sky by pieces of advanced capitalist machinery whose remoteness from the scene of murder is itself a mockery of the desire of the victims for immediate proximity—to real revolution, to other human beings, to the actuality of their own ideals, etc. Is this a paradox? In Bloomsbury I had dinner with an old Trotskyist friend who said his proudest achievement in life was that he once got ambushed and beaten unconscious in Leeds by members of Combat 18. Was he answering my question? I doubt that Sean Bonney knew why it was that he thought his line about cutting the throats of Tories in the street was the most peaceful thing he'd ever written; but where would the poetry have been in the idea that it was the most violent?

I'm saying that uncertainty, inconclusiveness, etc., is a moment of total irrefutable commitment, and not its opposite. I know that that's an obvious thing to assert, but it provides me with some initial terms with which to think about the last poem that Sean posted on his blog, about three weeks before his death:

Confession 2

while people are starving, wealth
is a crime. I am not willing to argue.
if you are hungry, no laws apply.
glass breaks easily. weapons
can be made from anything.
crime should not go unpunished.

the meaning of royalty

it too can be killed[6]

It's a scene in which absolutely everything has been stripped away. Nothing is left, no grand theories, no beautiful vision, no historical process. All the spatters and circumvolutions of the earlier collages are gone, the purples and lurid pinks come back in greyscale, "no way to know how or where or when — or if — he died, exactly," and what remains is hatred of the rich, the last thing it is possible to clutch onto once every other reality has crumbled or been rejected, and the refusal of explanation: "I am not willing to argue." And you could read this as a quintessential "last poem," a self-portrait of the artist holding onto his one remaining certainty after everything else has gone up in smoke: Sean Bonney presents the essence of his system, the moral ground-zero across which all of the stray dogs and political assassins and ridiculous nymphs and nasty waifs and burning comets of his imagination pass like plastic bags in the wind. I don't think that's what it is though. Sean's poetry was always unwilling to argue. It was always full of declarations about what constituted a waste of his, and our, time. His historical poetry replaced 99% of the present with an enormous yawning ellipsis. It could never have been such a mad fucking kick if it didn't. He showed us that poetry should be willing to come out and say straight up and as bluntly as any one-minute punk song that their reality is DEAD and that if you want to ask who they are then you've already missed the point. Of course they fucking owe us a living. And if we can't say it in those terms then we shouldn't bother writing poetry, and everything we can pay to learn in an MFA class is just mimicry of the official technique for smashing a teenaged protestor's head against a pavement, as you know. "Intelligibility is as much to be feared as desired."

I want to describe a relation in Sean's poetry that I find hard to get down. I know that I've written to you about this already,

---

6   Sean Bonney, "Confession 2," *Abandoned Buildings*, October 20, 2019, http://abandonedbuildings.blogspot.com/2019/10/confession-2.html; emphasis in original.

but in my own life in the last year or so I've felt myself being pulled further and further away from my earlier conceptual and political certainties. As I have come to know more about my immediate social environment, about the state and the real lives of the people I live around, and as more of my friends have died, become sick, or have broken down, the idea of simple political solutions to suffering have filled me with more and more nausea. I have wanted more and more intensely to write from within this state, from within the suffering that I experience vicariously, and not to conjure for my own benefit some fantastic alluring exit from it. I've wanted to write about the immediacy of being stuck, dying, sick, or mentally imploded, and I began to hate any art that feeds those experiences into some machine that we can call Marxism, or revolutionary politics. I have tried to live in this immediacy and to speak and fight for it, to love it as the material of working-class art, in which we can say, here is the speech of the streets and the vernacular, and of the pain and the pleasure of the parties and prison visits and the heat and zero-hour contracts: and here you are. And can you respond to it? And can you recognize its power? And in some ways this movement in my thinking has felt like progress to me; and sometimes it has felt like recession, and fear and disappointment and cowardice filter into it and are taken up on its currents and poison it like a kind of middle-class lead contamination, and I feel how easily it can be denatured into reaction, insularity, and mean-spiritedness, another version of the pig-headedness that can only understand someone's decision to fight for world revolution in a place they have never been in terms of the events of that person's early childhood, or its consequences for the warm nurturing space of a now-bereft nuclear family.

The last lines of his poetry that Sean published are a dictionary definition: "the meaning of royalty." They continue a tradition in his writing, of establishing step-by-step an alternative system of meanings, a dual-power structure in the English language itself: "the alphabet was a system of blackmail / complacent, would skate on our regulated senses"; "screams of contempt and pain, lodged in [...] the centre of our names."⁷ Open almost any of his books at random and you find statements like this. They are so essential to his poetry. None of our words can mean what they mean by them; to the extent that they do, our avant-garde writing may as well be an internal memorandum on a computer in the Home Office. We all write from a place that relegates us all: anyone who thinks that the British state is in Whitehall and is not also a slick of mucus at the back of their own throat has a very limited understanding of what art and politics is.⁸

And the poetry returns all the time to this baseline. Lots of people have said and will say that his writing was full of astonishing metaphors. But that's a kind of failure of response. As a poet, Sean treated metaphors as definitions. His use of the word "is" is confrontational: if he tells you that "fire is physical time," he means that it is not "the flames, light and heat, and often smoke, that are produced when something burns."⁹ Negativity runs through the writing like indistinct figures through a tunnel, and the sound of their footsteps echoes throughout even the most inventive of its passages and constitutes his type of rhythm and blues. In my mind the movement is always towards a new kind of writing degree zero, the concrete literality of a language no one has ever spoken and that no one ever will, way out beyond the exercises of literary criticism that when you really get down to it are just another version of CPS barristers trying to explain drill music to a judge. "I am not willing to argue" also means "I will do nothing but define"; and there is no more anarchistic commitment in Sean's writing than that. "We must consciously create our own world, not according to mindless customs and

---

7   Sean Bonney, "Happiness: Poems after Rimbaud," in *Happiness: Poems after Rimbaud* (London: Unkant, 2011), 13; *Ghosts* (London: Materials, 2017), n.p.
8   "What do protests, purpling flowers, starlings, police and endless daylight have in common? I write from a place that relegates us all."
9   "fire is physical time. is absolute unrest" ("Happiness: Poems after Rimbaud," 22). See also "this eschews metaphor, the enemy / 'is', a defining molecule" (34).

destructive prejudices, but according to the canons of reason, reflection and discourse that uniquely belong to our own species." Again: if you meet a Tory in the street, cut his throat. Two ways of saying the same thing, to be asserted simultaneously, in the manner of Sean's syllabi from the period just before the financial crisis. "HEX ENDUCTION HOUR (The Fall) and/or FUCK DE BOERE (Peter Brotzmann) to be listened to only while reading ROSA LUXEMBURG /// The Accumulation of Capital."

So here is the dynamic that that way of thinking helps me to overcome: we feel we have to disobey everything else in order to see at all,[10] and the stale formulae of radical politics produce in us a kind of overwhelming revulsion, and we return to the world in search of new experience, and over time the immediacies that we learn to articulate become formulae of a new variety, and our repudiation of the alleged identity of "unwillingness to argue" and mental deprivation segues into a new conservatism on a reduced scale, into stubborn possessive smallness, refusal to accept loss, tired anti-intellectualism, hatred of sudden upheaval, and obsessive fear of dying, which is to say into the entire range of curtain-twitching pathology that can be attributed to the average English voter as their birthright and common inheritance. This is the path of hatred for empty ideas that is so necessary to poetry and that nevertheless terminates over and over again in… some new empty ideas. And what I want to explain is how Sean's poetry contains another route that closely resembles this one but isn't it, and which I want to be able to define for myself more consistently (I think of Anne Boyer on what resembles the grave but isn't).

Or perhaps that's too strong. Sometimes we don't start out by wanting to disobey everything but by just feeling exhausted, done. The times when I have felt the most sickened by my own formulae are the times when I have felt most acutely that they do nothing for those who are closest to me. Our ABCs, our smart

---

10 "To see and experience the ways in which we are impossible without one another is to be convinced that we must disobey everything else in order to see at all."

turns of phrase, all the dumb shit that we have said to ourselves, our belief in rhetoric or symbols or beautiful argument, everything that is vivid or life-giving in our minds becomes ugly in the face of its inability to change even the most basic things about our own lives and the lives of the people we care about. We return into ourselves: "everything forced to the surface. I don't feel I'm myself anymore. I've fallen to pieces, I can hardly breathe. My body has become something else, has fled into its smallest dimensions, has scattered into zero. And yet, as soon as it got to that, it took a deep breath, it could suddenly do it, it had passed across, it could see its indeterminable function within the whole." And learning to compose like that from the "smallest dimensions" of ourselves is something that Sean worked on constantly for the last ten years. This moment from Brecht about "passing across" was a total obsession for him: the trial of his poetry is always to find in the last thing we have left a power of expression that is greater than the sum total of everything that has been taken away. "The very simplest words / must be enough. When I say what things are like / everyone's heart must be torn to shreds." "Thatcher faked her death." "Put your shoes on, get started / someone will finish." It's for that reason that the tributes to Sean written after his death that have hurt me the most are always the most syntactically atomized. Take what Verity Spott wrote: "My friend. Our friend. Our comrade. Our ridiculous man. Our ghosts. Our poetries. Our eternal fires, winds and reveries. Sean Bonney. Love." Tim Thornton: "how I wonder what we are." It's all there, the complex expression of simple class hatred, the moment of action in the scene of destitution ("weapons / can be made from anything"), the ability to make exhaustion into a power of negativity (never work/never argue), the discovery of a totally alternative universe in a poetry that does nothing more than — that can do nothing more than — define its own words, and the cynicism and bliss and inextinguishable hilarity of all this, and the delight in brokenness: "glass breaks easily." Most things break easily. Language breaks easily. Most poetry is wretched not because language is hard to break but because people are afraid to break it, so break it. don't argue. just fucking break it. stop killing yourself.

I'll try to summarize.

I've tended to think that what I have taught myself to reject is false arguments about political life, in favor of a sober recognition of what is in front of me. I have found this way of thinking liberating, and it has also led me inexorably towards depression and a kind of political paralysis.

I now realize that I had in mind at the same time another kind of development that needs to be independently defined. This is rejection of argument on their terms, in favor not of the world as it is, but of self-definition. The former thinking involves a kind of retreat into the self and its circle of intimate attachments. The latter involves an affirmation of the self by means of its reclamation from a world that immiserates it. It says, I will not waste my time on this. We will have our own definition of royalty, as well as of what it means to kill it. It says fuck the pigs at this moment and throughout all eternity.

And this is the relation that I have needed Sean's poetry to clarify for me. I want to state it plainly because I am not certain that I can prevent myself from forgetting it: the poetry of our self-definition seems always to be receding into the poetry of our disillusionment. The "idealism vs. realism" conflict (somewhere else you call it "the world as I experience it" vs. "how I'd like it to look, feel, run")[11] is a travesty of the greater conflict in our lives, and yet it constantly reasserts itself over it. Its capacity for reassertion is the most important thing about it. It is so hard to get free of it. It is so much easier to imagine a "real world" and some realm of empty ideas that falsifies it than it is to say convincingly that I am not willing to argue, because the first way of thinking is just an inert conceptual model whereas the second is an attitude and a trial and in its own small way a point

---

11 Lotte L.S., "Strange Country: On Ai, Frank Stanford, and Page Expectations," *Riggwelter,* February 4, 2019, https://riggwelterpress.wordpress.com/2019/02/04/strange-country-on-ai-frank-stanford-and-page-expectations/.

of no return; and the attitude (Kirill Medvedev might call it the "noise")[12] is always dying out, daily, leaving the model behind it, like the sketch of a body on a pavement. Here is the death-mask for our own living hatred of empty ideas. And I fucking love this last poem by Sean because every time I read it I see in its absolute fatigue and disillusionment a way out, into the smallest dimensions of itself and across into the realization that this is how I have always wanted my life to sound.

•

> To never truly be convinced by the act of naming (and thereby writing) is to forever do a double take on my own intentions. Names individualise the context in which we think and act together, and yet to write of an undisclosed "we" — whether "for," "with," "about," or "to" — is to represent, one way or another. Why claim words that belong to us all? It is an anarchist tradition to disbelieve copyright or ownership, to refuse to talk on behalf of the group, to reject an identified and uniformed set of desires or ideals. To recognise that our thoughts and desires are the products of numerous people, but not some cognate "movement" or homogenous group — not a "group" at all.

I am more interested in celebrating Sean's ability to liberate us from everything that is pointless and constipated in our culture than in mourning his disappearance from it. In my mind, poetry is a kind of street party that runs through all the wars and pandemics and Tory Party conferences and unfulfilled desires and suicides and breakdowns and out the other side; and no one gets into it unless they admit to themselves they can say anything they fucking like; and the only thing you ever learn here is that that's the only thing there is to do. I started to write poems

---

12 Kirill Medvedev, "My Fascism (A Few Truths)," in *It's No Good*, ed. Keith Gessen, trans. Keith Gessen with Mark Krotov, Cory Merrill, and Bela Shayevich (New York: Ugly Duckling Presse/N+1, 2012), 145.

only when I first realized this (late), and Sean just reminded me that I'll realize it again before I write my last one too. It's a law of nature, just like wealth is a crime.

But I said earlier that I'd say something about the rules you set out for talking about who "we" are (about who your "group that is not a group" is). The question of naming runs through the whole of the poem, but the passage that I quoted above from the "p.s." has the sense of a conclusion: "It is an anarchist tradition to disbelieve copyright or ownership, to refuse to talk on behalf of the group, to reject an identified and uniformed set of desires or ideals. To recognise that our thoughts and desires are the products of numerous people, but not some cognate 'movement' or homogenous group — not a 'group' at all." I feel like you kind of end up — maybe there's a better word for it than this — falling back on this assertion? Why should we expect anarchist "traditions" to solve any of our problems? — since they haven't done such a good job up until now — and yet that's also why the claim seems true to me. I've been searching in my head for weeks for a phrase to describe the overtone in it, the noise that it makes, and it's only now that I realize stupidly and with a feeling almost of embarrassment that one of the reasons why the passage stood out to me in the first place is that that sound, of a mind falling back on its principles and refusing to budge, is the same sound that you get in "Confession 2." I'm not willing to argue. And then I think of a structure of thought that I associate with the poetry of Lisa Jeschke: better to be blurry and forgettable than crisp and immediately perceptible. Better to fall back on an argument than make it. Better to be a living person struggling to hold on to a scrap of meaning than a corpse drowned in a sea of it. Better the anarchist tradition of refusing to talk on behalf of the group — and better its crudest rule of thumb about how to conduct yourself in a street protest — than even the most cleverly sophisticated intellectual tradition of cravenly selling it out. Like Sean would have said, it's obvious. If we want to write useful poems, we have to keep on reminding ourselves of how it feels to refuse to step out of the road. Of course one of the ways to do that is actually to refuse to do it.

Poetry is the street party that runs through the middle of an unconscionable reality / argument is the court order that proscribes it. I have found in my own life that the less willing we are to debate, the more we're able to say, and I've spent so much time arguing about this here that I've hardly said anything about what your poem contains and invokes: things that people have said to us. Little slivers of conversation coming free from their times and places, floating instances, plastic chairs, community notice boards, bedrooms, the non-developmental spaces in our lives, lights moving across the walls, orange hesitating to pink in the hospital receptions and reception centers, one feeling wrapped around another, and the way that these realities seem to move away from us as we step towards them, as the mirages of our anti-capitalism; and "what could happen if we just left [them] alone?"[13] The obvious implication is that we feel some compulsion to do something to them (to argue about them? to fuck them up and mis-describe them?) because these are the kinds of persons we are, and these are the lives that we lead: "happens in floating instances," and other semi-anagrams for the word happiness.[14] I will never feel truly certain about my ability to talk about things that can only be seen when they are left slightly out of focus, "poems after Rimbaud," flowers, protests, starlings, daylight, the nineteenth century, Regents Street or Jupiter, an unwanted phone call and the glass window between the lifts and the corridor of the secure ward, drunken speech and the need to trash sentiment whose title could be "the

---

13 "voices rising up from the back / of the room / singing / 'no, I don't want you to turn his death / into a theatre performance / funded by the state' / not everything must become 'art,' / become 'cause,' become transformed — what could happen if you just left it alone?"

14 "Happens in floating instances / that yellow / and dampen / a hindsight that differs / depending on who is looking / a group which never actually admitted / to being a group / so out of tune / with the spinning singing of the world [...]"

absence /"[15] or sunlight through an eyelid or our class enemies or the "UK general election of 2019" in the meridian of its conjugations of displaced feeling. And can I hold on to it? And can I prevent myself from destroying it? For me, the important difference is not between this state that I am now gesturing toward with a list of nouns and "clarity." That would just be the ideal vs. reality protocol again. It's the difference between that feeling and the feeling of sprinting onto a runway to stop a plane taking off. We need both. There will always be spaces in which we are left behind. There are always ways to pass back out of them in a blur. We love the people who have shown us it is possible.

Brussels 1872 / London 2020: here are some of my instinctual aversions. I don't want to talk about memories. I don't want to talk about "my" past. I don't want to talk about the places where we drank or community centers or listservs or how much care it took on the part of the people I have written about to persuade me that I could do what I am now doing. I pass through periods of thinking our political rulers are hateful distorted fascists who deserve to be assassinated and periods of thinking they are quite normal, unremarkable people whose lives are so tedious I can't even bring myself to name them, and the sensation of this uncertainty is more valuable to me than any conceivable state of elucidation. I spend my day trying to write a few sentences about this, and I wake up in the middle of the night from a nightmare in which the idea of a decade is something solid and impermeable and looming until the 5 a.m. air comes in through the window and dispels it. And like you I want to say "fuck you" to the deadening influence of remembrance, and to plant that "fuck you" like a flower in a landscape where the light is incapable of failing, and like you I both can and cannot do it.

oh well.

---

15 "old NASA training camps / the absence / of landmarks" [...]

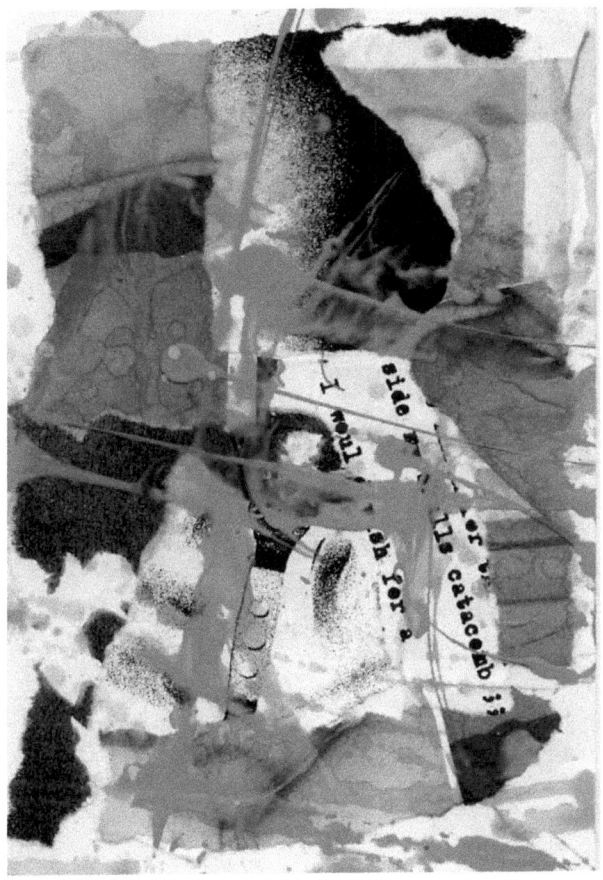

Fig. 1. Sean Bonney, Baudelaire Collage, September 2006.
Courtesy of the Estate of Sean Bonney.

Bibliography

Adorno, Theodor, and Max Horkheimer. *The Dialectic of Enlightenment.* Translated by John Cumming. London: Verso, 1979.

Anonymous. "Some Communal Thoughts on Poetry and Anti-fascist Culture." *Poetry Emergency: A North West Radical Poetry Festival,* November 23–24, 2018. https://poetryemergency.files.wordpress.com/2019/05/some-communal-thoughts-on-poetry-and-anti-fascist-culture-1.pdf.

Baraka, Amiri [LeRoi Jones]. *The System of Dante's Hell: A Novel.* New York: Grove Press, 1966.

———. *Transbluesency: The Selected Poems of Amiri Baraka/LeRoi Jones (1961–1995).* Edited by Paul Vangelisti. New York: Marsilio Publishers, 1995.

Barrie, Joshua. "Read the Heartbreaking Poems of a Man Who Committed Suicide after Working in a Foxconn Factory." *Business Insider UK,* November 6, 2014. http://uk.businessinsider.com/foxconn-factory-workers-suicide-poems-2014-11.

BBC News. "Thomas Mair: Extremist loner who targeted Jo Cox." *BBC,* November 23, 2016. http://www.bbc.co.uk/news/uk-38071894.

BBC Panorama: "The Nailbomber." *BBC,* June 30, 2000. http://news.bbc.co.uk/hi/english/static/audio_video/programmes/panorama/transcripts/transcript_30_06_00.txt.

BBC Radio 1Xtra. "Novelist Freestyle for Toddla T (Part 2)." *YouTube,* February 6, 2018. https://www.youtube.com/watch?v=TwjR184wVGQ.

Benjamin, Walter. "The Work of Art in the Age of Its Mechanical Reproduction." In *The Work of Art in the Age of Its Technological Reproducibility: And Other Writings on Media,* edited by Michael W. Jennings, Brigid Doherty, and Thomas Y. Levine, 19–55. Cambridge: Harvard University Press, 2008.

Berlant, Lauren. *Cruel Optimism.* Durham: Duke University Press, 2011.

Bersani, Leo. *Is the Rectum a Grave? And Other Essays.* Chicago: University of Chicago Press, 2009.

Beynon, Lucy, and Lisa Jeschke. *David Cameron: A Theatre of Knife Songs.* Cambridge: Shit Valley, 2015.

Bonney, Sean. "Confession 2." *Abandoned Buildings,* October 20, 2019. http://abandonedbuildings.blogspot.com/2019/10/confession-2.html.

——— . *Ghosts.* London: Materials, 2017.

——— . *Happiness: Poems after Rimbaud.* London: Unkant, 2011.

Boyer, Anne. "Clickbait Thanatos: On the Poetics of Post-Privacy." In *A Handbook of Disappointed Fate,* 113–18. New York: Ugly Duckling Presse, 2018.

——— . *Garments against Women.* London: Mute, 2016.

Brecht, Bertolt. *The Measures Taken and Other Lehrstücke.* New York: Arcade Publishing, 2001.

Cage, John. "Overpopulation and Art." In *Composed in America,* edited by Marjorie Perloff and Charles Junkerman, 14–38. Chicago: University of Chicago Press, 1994.

Cortez, Jayne. *Coagulations: New and Selected Poems.* London: Pluto, 1985.

———. "Supersurrealist Vision: Interview with Jayne Cortez." In *Heroism in the New Black Poetry: Introductions and Interviews*, edited by D.H. Melham, 181–211. Lexington: University of Kentucky Press, 1990.

Crawford, Alejandro Miguel Justino. *Diana Hamilton's Dreams*. Oakland: Gauss PDF, 2016. https://gausspdf.itch.io/dhd.

Davidson, Miri. "Election Diary." In *How to Win*, edited by Tories Out. London: Tories Out, 2020. https://tories-out-propaganda-unit.tumblr.com/.

Davies-Kumadiro, Beth. "Eugenics Is Not a Fringe Issue — It Influences UK Immigration Policy." *Novara Media,* January 13, 2018. https://novaramedia.com/2018/01/13/eugenics-is-not-a-fringe-issue-it-influences-uk-immigration-policy/.

Debord, Guy. *Panegyric, Volumes 1 & 2*. Translated by James McHale. London: Verso, 2004.

DIS Magazine. "DISCREET Call for Participants." *discover: the dis blog,* April 11, 2016. http://dismagazine.com/blog/81659/discreet-call-for-participants/.

———. "Laboria Cuboniks in Conversation." *discover: the dis blog,* July 23, 2016. http://dismagazine.com/blog/81953/laboria-cuboniks-in-conversation/.

Dou, Eva. "After Suicide, Foxconn Worker's Poems Strike a Chord." *The Wall Street Journal,* November 7, 2014. http://blogs.wsj.com/chinarealtime/2014/11/07/after-suicide-foxconn-workers-poems-strike-a-chord/.

Eliot, T.S. *Collected Poems, 1909–1962*. New York: Harcourt, Brace & World, 1963.

Fanon, Frantz. *The Wretched of the Earth*. Translated by Constance Farrington. London: Penguin, 1961.

Foxconn Technology Group. "2014 Social and Environmental Responsibility Report." June 2015. https://www.honhai.com/s3/reports/CSR%E5%A0%B1%E5%91%8A%E6%9B%B8/%E8%8B%B1%E6%96%87%E7%89%88/2014%20CSR%20report.pdf.

Freud, Sigmund. "The Splitting of the Ego in the Process of Defence." In *The Complete Psychological Works of Sigmund*

Freud, edited by James Strachey et al., Volume 23, 275–79. London: Vintage, 2001.

Frost, Jackqueline. *The Third Event: Parts 1 & 2.* Cambridge: Tipped Press, 2018.

———. *The Third Event: Part Three.* London: Crater, 2019.

Grundy, David. "'As Life is to Other Themes': Ian Heames' Sonnets." *Streams of Expression,* September 9, 2015. http://streamsofexpression.blogspot.com/2015/09/as-life-is-to-other-themes-ian-heames.html.

———. "David Grundy's Intro to My Cambridge Reading." *Gods of the Plague,* March 14, 2018. https://godsoftheplague.tumblr.com/post/171865396568/david-grundys-intro-to-my-cambridge-reading.

———. "Sean Bonney's Life Work." *Poetry Foundation,* March 9, 2020. https://www.poetryfoundation.org/harriet/2020/03/sean-bonneys-life-work.

Hayward, Danny. "Questions for an Anti-Fascist Culture (Nov. 2018)." https://bit.ly/2RwDpin.

———. "Tradition vs. Grid: Simone White's Dear Angel of Death." *Texte zur Kunst* 117 (March 2020): 168–76.

Hille, Kathrin. "Foxconn to Raise Salaries 20% after Suicides." *The Financial Times,* May 28, 2010. http://www.ft.com/cms/s/2/5e1ee750-6a05-11df-a978-00144feab49a.html.

Hong, Bendon. "The Eerie Poetry of Chinese Suicide Victims." *Vice Online*, November 14, 2014. https://www.vice.com/en_uk/read/death-poems-are-a-thing-in-china-right-now.

Iadarola, Alexander. "Interview with Game Designer Porpentine Charity Heartscape." *Mask Magazine,* May 29, 2017. http://www.maskmagazine.com/the-greatest-hits-issue/work/porpentine-charity-heartscape-reprise.

Jackson, George. *Soledad Brother: The Prison Letters of George Jackson.* Chicago: Lawrence Hill Books, 1994.

Kruk, Frances. *Lo-Fi Frags In-Progress.* London: Veer Books, 2015.

Lee, Siri. "Game Review: the shape you make when you want your bones to be closest to the surface." *Critical Videogames*

Studies, October 16, 2018. https://uofcmediastudies.wixsite.com/vgs2018/blog/game-review-the-shape-you-make-when-you-want-your-bones-to-be-closest-to-the-surface.

Jeschke, Lisa. "From *The Anthology of Poems by Drunk Women.*" In *Look at Hazards, Look at Losses,* edited by Group for Conceptual Politics, Danny Hayward, Anthony Iles, Lisa Jeschke, Benjamin Noys, Eirik Steinhoff, and Marina Vishmidt, 119–33. London: Mute Publishing, 2017.

———. *The Anthology of Poems by Drunk Women.* Cambridge: Materials, 2018.

L.S., Lotte. "'Not to speak about / only to speak nearby.'" *Poetry Foundation Blog,* May 13, 2019. https://www.poetryfoundation.org/harriet/2019/05/not-to-speak-about-only-to-speak-nearby.

———. "Strange Country: On Ai, Frank Stanford, and Page Expectations." *Riggwelter,* February 4, 2019. https://riggwelterpress.wordpress.com/2019/02/04/strange-country-on-ai-frank-stanford-and-page-expectations/.

———. *A town, three cities, a fig, a riot, two blue hyacinths, three beginnings, five letters, a "death", two solitudes, façades, four loose dogs, a doppelgänger, a likeness, three airport floors, thirty-six weeks...* Tripwire Pamphlet Series #10. https://tripwirejournal.com/tripwire-pamphlet-series/.

Lazzarato, Maurizio. *The Making of the Indebted Man: An Essay on the Neoliberal Condition.* Translated by Joshua David Jordan. Los Angeles: Semiotext(e), 2012.

Luxemburg, Rosa. *The Accumulation of Capital.* Translated by Agnes Schwarzschild. London: Routledge, 2003.

MacSweeney, Barry. *Wolf Tongue: Selected Poems 1965–2000.* Newcastle: Bloodaxe, 2003.

Marx, Karl. *A Contribution to the Critique of Political Economy.* Translated by N.I. Stone. Chicago: Charles H. Kerr, 1904.

———. *Capital, Volume I.* In *Collected Works of Marx and Engels,* Volume 35. London: Lawrence & Wishart, 2010.

———. *Critique of the Gotha Program.* In *Collected Works of Marx and Engels,* Volume 24. London: Lawrence & Wishart, 2010.

Mason, Paul. *Postcapitalism: A Guide to Our Future.* London: Penguin, 2015.

MayDay Rooms. "Sam Solomon and Lisa Jeschke – Materials Poetry Reading Series." *YouTube,* March 18, 2018. https://www.youtube.com/watch?v=usAzYW10wdM.

———. "The Decline and Fall of the Home Office." *YouTube,* September 28, 2018. https://www.youtube.com/watch?v=YKGUZNtF878

Mayer, Bernadette. *Sonnets.* New York: Tender Buttons Press, 2014.

Medvedev, Kirill. "My Fascism (A Few Truths)." In *It's No Good,* edited by Keith Gessen, translated by Keith Gessen with Mark Krotov, Cory Merrill, and Bela Shayevich, 117–49. New York: Ugly Duckling Presse/N+1, 2012.

Megaw, Nicholas. "Britain's Priory Group Sold to US Healthcare Company for £1.5bn." *Financial Times,* January, 4 2016. https://www.ft.com/content/0fa13fe2-b2e3-11e5-b147-e5e5bba42e51.

Mehri, Momtaza. "Letters from a Young (Female) Poet." *The Millions,* January 31, 2018. https://themillions.com/2018/01/letters-from-a-young-female-poet.html.

Mohandesi, Salar, and Asad Haider. "Workers' Inquiry: A Genealogy." *Viewpoint Magazine,* September 27, 2013. https://www.viewpointmag.com/2013/09/27/workers-inquiry-a-genealogy/.

Nagle, Angela. *Kill All Normies: Online Culture Wars from 4Chan and Tumblr to Trump and the Alt-Right.* Winchester: Zero Books, 2017.

Nairn, Tom. *The Left against Europe?* Harmondsworth: Penguin, 1973.

Nao. "The Poetry and Brief Life of a Foxconn Worker: Xu Lizhi (1990–2014)." *Libcom.org,* October 29, 2014. https://libcom.org/blog/xulizhi-foxconn-suicide-poetry.

O'Hara, Frank. *Lunch Poems.* San Francisco: City Lights Books, 2014.

———. *The Collected Poems of Frank O'Hara.* Edited by Donald Allen. Berkeley: University of California Press, 1995.

Peled, Avi. *NeuroAnalysis: Bridging the Gap between Neuroscience, Psychoanalysis and Psychiatry.* London: Routledge, 2008.

Pole Vault. "David Cameron: A Theatre of Knife-Songs, Lisa Jeschke & Lucy Beynon, 26 June 2014, Turbamento @ The Betsy Trotwood." *YouTube,* February 9, 2015. https://www.youtube.com/watch?v=1uhG7iOAmoE

———. "THE TRAGEDY OF THERESA MAY." *YouTube,* July 12, 2016. https://www.youtube.com/watch?v=djwyIRJ3DWE.

Porpentine Charity Heartscape. *Everything You Swallow Will One Day Come Up Like a Stone.* http://storycade.com/everythingyouswallow/. Website currently defunct.

———. *the shape you make when you want your bones to be closest to the surface. Slime Daughter,* 2018. http://www.slimedaughter.com/games/twine/closest.

———. *With Those We Love Alive. Slime Daughter,* 2014. http://slimedaughter.com/games/twine/wtwla/.

PricewaterhouseCoopers. "The Sharing Economy." *Consumer Intelligence Series.* 2015. https://www.pwc.com/us/en/technology/publications/assets/pwc-consumer-intelligence-series-the-sharing-economy.pdf.

Raha, Nat. *Of Sirens / Body and Faultlines.* London: Veer Books, 2016.

———. *Of Sirens, Body & Faultlines.* Norwich: Boiler House Press, 2018.

———. "[Of Sirens / Body & Faultlines] Second Edition / Readings: Small Publishers Fair, Brighton with M. Nourbese Philip." *Sociopathetic Semaphores,* November 5, 2015. http://sociopatheticsemaphores.blogspot.com/2015/11/of-sirens-body-faultlines-second.html.

Reed, Ishmael. "Badman of the Guest Professor." In *Every Goodbye Ain't Gone: An Anthology of Innovative Poetry by African Americans,* edited by Aldon Lynn Neilson and Lauri Ramey, 213–17. Tuscaloosa: University of Alabama Press, 2006.

Reich, Wilhelm. *The Mass Psychology of Fascism.* Translated by Mary Boyd Higgins. Harmondsworth: Penguin, 1970.

Ren, Hao, et al. "Factory Stories: On the Conditions and Struggles in Chinese Workplaces." *Gongchao.org*, 2012–2015. http://www.gongchao.org/en/factory-stories

Rimbaud, Arthur. *Rimbaud Complete*. Translated by Wyatt Mason. New York: Modern Library, 2003.

Roberts, Dexter. "The Rise of a Chinese Worker's Movement." *Bloomberg Weekly*, June 10, 2010. https://www.bloomberg.com/news/articles/2010-06-10/the-rise-of-a-chinese-workers-movement,

Rogers, Carl R. *On Becoming a Person: A Therapist's View of Psychotherapy*. Boston: Houghton-Mifflin, 1961.

Rowbotham, Sheila. *Promise of a Dream: Remembering the Sixties*. London: Verso, 2002.

Rowthorn, Bob. *The Costs and Benefits of Large-Scale Immigration*. London: Civitas, 2015.

———. "The Politics of the Alternative Economic Strategy." *Marxism Today* (January 1981): 4–10. http://banmarchive.org.uk/collections/mt/pdf/81_01_04.pdf.

Rymbu, Galina. "Language Wrecker." Translated by Joan Brooks. *Two Lines* 27 (Fall 2017). *Center for the Art of Translation Online Exclusive*. https://www.catranslation.org/online-exclusive/language-wrecker/.

Serge, Victor. *Notebooks 1936–1947*. Translated by Mitchell Abidor and Richard Greenman. New York: New York Review of Books, 2019.

Silberman, Steve. *Neurotribes: The Legacy of Autism and the Future of Neurodiversity*. New York: Penguin Random House, 2015.

Smith, Jason E. "Nowhere to Go: Automation, Then and Now." *The Brooklyn Rail*, March 2017. http://brooklynrail.org/2017/03/field-notes/Nowhere-to-Go.

Sollfrank, Cornelia, and Rachel Baker. "Revisiting the Future with Laboria Cuboniks: A Conversation." *Furtherfield*, July 27, 2016. http://www.furtherfield.org/features/interviews/revisiting-future-laboria-cuboniks-conversation.

Sorel, Georges. *Reflections on Violence*. Edited by Jeremy Jennings. Cambridge: Cambridge University Press, 1999.

SovietFilms. "MARGARET THATCHER DEAD!! Brixton Celebrates Party – Ghost Town." *YouTube,* April 9, 2013. https://www.youtube.com/watch?v=ikhRGrJReJ8.

Sparrow, Norbert, and Rainer Werner Fassbinder, "'I Let the Audience Feel and Think': An Interview with Rainer Werner Fassbinder." *Cinéaste* 8, no. 2 (1977): 20–21. https://www.jstor.org/stable/41685803.

Spillett, Richard. "'Jekyll and Hyde' Assassin Was a Loner Who Scoured Himself with Brillo Pads Because of Cleanliness Obsession and Spent His Life on Mental Health Drugs." *Daily Mail,* November 23, 2016. http://www.dailymail.co.uk/news/article-3960988/Jekyll-Hyde-Jo-Cox-assassin-Thomas-Mair.html.

Spott, Verity. *Click Away Close Door Say.* London: Contraband, 2017.

———. "Gender Dysphoria." *Two Torn Halves,* March 13, 2016. http://twotornhalves.blogspot.co.uk/2016/03/gender-dysphoria.html

———. *Gideon.* Brighton: Barque Press, 2014.

———. *Trans* Manifestos.* Cambridge: Shit Valley, 2016.

———. "We Make Things Possible." *Prelude Mag* 3 (2016). https://preludemag.com/issues/3/we-make-this-possible/.

Srnicek, Nick, and Alex Williams. *Inventing the Future: Postcapitalism and a World without Work.* London: Verso, 2015.

Sutherland, Keston. "Blocks: Form Since the Crash — A Seminar at New York University, 13 November 2015." *Internet Archive.* https://archive.org/details/BlocksSeminarAtNYU13November2015.

———. *Poetical Works 1999–2015.* London: Enitharmon Press, 2015.

———. *Whither Russia.* Brighton: Barque Press, 2017.

Sutherland, Keston, and John Tamplin. "Transcription of a Conversation in Princeton, U.S.A., 7th December 2015." *Black Box Manifold* 17 (Winter 2016). http://www.manifold.group.shef.ac.uk/issue17/KestonSutherlandJohnTamplinBM17.html.

Tharoor, Ishaan. "The Haunting Poetry of a Chinese Factory Worker Who Committed Suicide." *The Washington Post*, November 12, 2014. https://www.washingtonpost.com/news/worldviews/wp/2014/11/12/the-haunting-poetry-of-a-chinese-factory-worker-who-committed-suicide/.

Theweleit, Klaus. *Male Fantasies*. 2 volumes. Minneapolis: University of Minnesota Press, 1987.

———. "Männliche Geburtsweisen." In *Das Land das Ausland heist: Essays, Reden, Interviews zu Politik und Kunst*, 2–27. Munich: Deutscher Taschenbuch Verlag, 1995.

Thompson, E.P. "Going into Europe." In *Writing by Candlelight*, 85–88. London: Merlin, 1980.

Thornton, Timothy. *Water and Burning Effects On/Off*. Cambridge: Shit Valley, 2015.

Time Staff. "Read Donald Trump's Full Inauguration Speech." *Time*, January 20, 2017. http://time.com/4640707/donald-trump-inauguration-speech-transcript/.

Van der Linden, Marcel M., and Gerald Hubmann. "Introduction." In *Marx's Capital: An Unfinishable Project?*, edited by Marcel M. van der Linden and Gerald Hubmann, 1–31. Leiden: Brill, 2018.

Wallace, Amanda. "Twine: Everything You Swallow Will One Day Come Up Like a Stone." *Storycade*, 2014. http://storycade.com/twine-everything-swallow-will-one-day-come-like-stone/.

Walters, Joanna. "Obama Departs White House with a Promise: 'I'll be right there with you.'" *The Guardian*, January 20, 2017. https://www.theguardian.com/us-news/2017/jan/20/barack-obama-departs-white-house.

Warner, Marina. "Learning My Lesson." *London Review of Books* 37, no. 6 (March 19, 2015). https://www.lrb.co.uk/the-paper/v37/n06/marina-warner/learning-my-lesson.

Watts, Rebecca. "The Cult of the Noble Amateur." *PN Review* 44, no. 3 (2018). https://www.pnreview.co.uk/cgi-bin/scribe?item_id=10090.

Wealth of Negations. "TERMS & CONDITIONS (Complete and unabridged)." *Wealth of Negations,* April 4, 2015. http://www.wealthofnegations.org.

White, Simone. *Dear Angel of Death.* New York: Ugly Duckling Presse, 2018.

Wieland, Christina. *The Undead Mother: Psychoanalytic Explorations of Masculinity, Femininity, and Matricide.* London: Karnac, 2000.

Winnicott, D.W. *Holding and Interpretation: Fragment of an Analysis.* Edited by M. Masud R. Khan. London: Hogarth Press, 1986.

Work and Pensions Committee. "Oral Evidence: The Department for Work and Pensions HC 997-I, Wednesday 11 May 2016." https://www.parliament.uk/globalassets/documents/commons-committees/work-and-pensions/160511-DWP.pdf.

Wright, Richard. *Native Son.* London: Vintage, 2000.

www.ingramcontent.com/pod-product-compliance
Lightning Source LLC
Chambersburg PA
CBHW071002160426
43193CB00012B/1888